Nigel McCrery worked as a policeman and investigated several murders before he left the force to become an undergraduate at Cambridge University. After being awarded an honours degree in History, he went on to work for the BBC Drama Department, with whom he still has a strong working relationship. Married with children, he lives in Nottingham.

Also by Nigel McCrery

Silent Witness
Strange Screams of Death
Spider's Web

ALL THE KING'S MEN

One of the Greatest Mysteries of the First World War Finally Solved

Nigel McCrery

LONDON · SYDNEY · NEW YORK · TOKYO · SINGAPORE · TORONTO

First published in Great Britain by Simon & Schuster UK Ltd, 1992
This edition first published by Pocket Books, 1999
An imprint of Simon & Schuster UK Ltd
A Viacom Company

1 3 5 7 9 10 8 6 4 2

Simon & Schuster UK Ltd
Africa House
64–78 Kingsway
London WC2B 6AH

Simon & Schuster Australia
Sydney

A CIP catalogue record for this book is available from the British Library

ISBN 0-671-01831-0

Printed and bound in Geat Britain by The Bath Press

To my mother
Julia Mary McCrery
In honour of my father
Colin George McCrery

(1928–1990)

Acknowledgements

Her Majesty the Queen.

His Royal Highness The Prince Edward; Amanda Hepton Paget; Hal Giblin; Peter Hiscocks; Graham Beck; Douglas Stott; Tom Cubitt; Edward Hunter; Ian Livesley; Hilary (Frenchy) Cook; Sir Julian Loyd, KCVO (former agent at Sandringham); John Pelly; Janet Fenwick; Robert Purdy; Kate Thaxton; Major Reeve; Michael Oswald, CVO; Eric Hancock; Fred Sturman; David White; Steve Clinch; Luke, Emily and Rebecca; Gill McCrery; Nevin Anthony; J.G. Parker; The Beck Collection; Madge Webber; the staff at Yarmouth Library, Norwich Library and King's Lynn Library; Imperial War Museum; Collingdale Newspaper Library; John Major (agent at Sandringham); workers on the Sandringham Estate; Dr Francis (Binky) Pattrick; Nigel Steel, Dept of Documents IWM; Peter Hart, Dept of Sound Records IWM; Dr Jay Winter; John Dawson; Jane Heard; Sir Christopher R. Proctor Beauchamp; Sir Robert Fellows; Geoff Crawford; Royal Archives at Windsor; Denis Ingle; Ashley McCrery; Anthony Beck; Norwich Cathedral; Gallipoli Association; Mary Stevens; Jim Isherwood; the staff at the Norfolk's Regimental Museum, Norwich; Alexandra Loch; F. Cripps; Gerald Gliddon; *Eastern Daily Press*; Alan Clay.

Contents

Illustrations xi

Foreword by Major General M.J.D. Walker, CBE xiii

Introduction 1

1 Before the Harvest 5

2 The Regiment 11

3 The Battalion 23

4 Goodbye-ee 37

5 Gallipoli: the Campaign 50

6 Foreign Fields 57

7 The Battle 68

8 The Aftermath 82

9 Corner of a Foreign Field 101

10 Strange Clouds 110

11 The Reason Why 114

12 A Final Farewell 120

My Officer 125

Appendix I: Officers that Travelled with the 1/5th Norfolks to Gallipoli 127

Appendix II: Casualties (other ranks) 1/5th Norfolks 12 August 1915 129

Appendix III: 1/5th Norfolks Regiment Territorials Prisoners-of-War during Gallipoli Campaign 135

Bibliography 137

Index 139

Illustrations

1. Sandringham House. 9
2. Officers and NCOs of the Sandringham Company. 18
3. Dereham Company route march 1915. 24
4. Lynn Company, King's Lynn market square 1914. 25
5. The Sandringham Company at Wolferton Camp 19 June 1912. 26
6. Lieutenant-Colonel Sir Horace Proctor-Beachamp. 27
7. Second-Lieutenant Montague Barclay Grenville Proctor-Beauchamp. 29
8. Albert Edward Alexander (Alec) Beck. 30
9. The Cubitt brothers. 32
10. Captain Edmund Gay. 34
11. Captain Arthur Devereux Pattrick. 35
12. Private Tom Williamson as a seventeen-year-old territorial. 41
13. King George V meeting Capt Frank Beck and the Sandringham Company at Colchester in November 1914. 44
14. Sandringham Company in tropical uniform 1915. 49
15. Map of the Gallipoli Peninsula. 51
16. Major Purdy. 62
17. Map of the battlefield. 69
18. Second-Lieutenant Rollo Pelly. 77
19. Officers of the 1/5th Battalion. 80
20. Newspaper report in the *Yarmouth Mercury* 16 October 1915. 84
21. His Royal Highness King George V with his Private Secretary, Stamfordham. 89
22. Prisoners-of-war in Constantinople, (sitting) Captain Coxon. 94

23. Her Majesty Queen Alexandra and Sir Dighton Probyn. 97
24. The Reverend Charles Pierrepoint Edwards. 102
25. Captain Frank Beck's watch. 108
26. Signaller Gordon Parker. 115
27. The Helles Memorial. 123

Foreword

by
Major General M.J.D. Walker CBE

Deputy Colonel (Norfolk Suffolk & Cambridgeshire)
The Royal Anglian Regiment

The British soldier and his officers have always sought adventure and roving and the off-chance that they may be able to lay down their lives for their country; no more so than when a major war has been at hand. Without these men British Regiments would not exist, nor would they have the fame and tradition which marks them apart from those in other armies of the world. Each regiment has a quality of its own. The Norfolks' reputation was enhanced by special charcteristics; a spirit of enterprise, a steadfastness in the face of adversity and a strong family bond all contributed to the will to succeed.

This story, involving the 5th battalion of territorials, brings all of these features into sharp focus; the patriotism and close comradeship of its officers and men; the quiet certainty that they were second to none and their determination to acquit themselves with distinction in circumstances of chaos and overwhelming odds. It gives a flavour, too, of the burden of grief suffered by the close-knit families at home.

It does more than bring a reasoned resolution to an unexplained incident during the campaign in the Dardanelles; it paints a picture of a British Infantry Regiment which I commend to all.

Introduction

Given the horror and slaughter of the First World War, normally the essential ingredients in the shaping of legends, there are surprisingly few instances of unexplained or mystical phenomena of the type from which myths develop and grow. The Angel of Mons, who is said to have appeared to troops during the bloody months of 1914 to give them comfort and hope to some people, indicated nothing short of divine intervention. Another example is the story of the 'Vanished Battalion'. On 12 August 1915, the 1/5th (territorial) battalion of the Norfolk Regiment vanished into the dust and smoke of a Gallipoli battle. Some reports say the whole regiment (some thousand men) disappeared whilst the official history contents itself with 250 officers and men. The legend has an authoritative source, no less a person than Sir Ian Hamilton, Commander-in-Chief in Gallipoli, who wrote of the incident in a despatch to Lord Kitchener: 'There happened a very mysterious thing ... They charged into the forest and were lost to sight or sound. Not one of them ever came back.'

Among the missing men of the 5th battalion was a company drawn exclusively from His Royal Highness King George V's country estate at Sandringham. Its ranks were made up of gardeners, gamekeepers, farm labourers and household servants and was led by the King's Agent at Sandringham, Capt Frank Beck. The loss of so many men close to the Royal Family prompted King George to enquire of Hamilton, 'What has happened to the Sandringham men?' Hamilton, despite lengthy enquiries was unable to throw any further light on the battalion's disappearance. The continuing search for the missing men involved the British Royal Family, the American and Turkish governments, the British Army, the Commonwealth War Graves Commission and a strange priest from an obscure island in Essex. At the end of the war in 1918 enquiries were made with the Turkish authorities to try to establish what had befallen the men, but they denied any knowledge of the missing Norfolks and were unable to shed any further light on their strange disappearance.

Over the years, the legend of the Vanished Battalion has grown and since the Second World War those protagonists of the Bermuda Triangle theory and of the existence of UFOs have, frequently and in several books and articles, put forward extra-terrestrial explanations. At an old comrades association meeting in 1965, held to celebrate the fiftieth anniversary of the Gallipoli landings, a former sapper of the New Zealand Expeditionary Forces gave his version of the disappearance of the 1/5th Norfolks. He related how he was in a sector overlooking the advance of the Norfolks and noticed some strange looking 'loaf of bread' shaped clouds on top of the hill (later versions say the clouds were shaped like a giant cross). He went on to say that 1/5th Norfolks marched into these clouds 'without hesitation'. About an hour later, shortly after the last of the troops had entered 'the clouds' they lifted off the ground rising slowly before moving off northward. When it had vanished from sight not a single Norfolk could be found, they had quite simply disappeared.

In 1919 under the foothills of the Tekke Tepe hills, close to where the 1/5th Norfolks had last fought and vanished, a mass grave was discovered by the Graves Registration Unit. It contained the bodies of a number of British soldiers. Some of these remains were identified as having been members of the Hampshire, Suffolk and Cheshire Regiments. The majority, however, were identifiable by their badges and insignia as belonging to the 1/5th Norfolks, although it was impossible to identify them individually. The remains of these men were removed to the Imperial War Graves Cemetery at Azmak, Suvla where they were reinterred. For the next seventy-five years the fate of the Norfolks remained shrouded in secrecy. What happened to the gallant Norfolks, and why has their fate been kept so secret for so long?

The history of the 5th Battalion and their final end is full of inconsistencies, so I have had to use my own judgement after examining the available evidence to explain what actually befell them. For the best part I believe my information to be correct, but I apologise in advance for any inadvertent mistakes. I hope that in this book I have at last answered the many questions relating to the strange disappearance of the 5th Norfolks. Who were they? Why were they sent to Gallipoli? And what finally befell the battalion during the futile fighting in that inhospitable Turkish peninsula? With the solving of this seventy-five-year old mystery may a very gallant band of gentlemen at last rest in peace.

Nigel McCrery
March 1992

Chapter one

Before the Harvest

The flowers left thick at nightfall in the wood
This Eastertide call into mind the men,
Now far from home, who, with their sweethearts, should
Have gathered them and will do never again.
Edward Thomas (1878-1917)

The attack was already a quarter of an hour late, the giant naval shells which had been whistling overhead on their way to the Turkish lines had stopped and an eerie unfamiliar silence had descended over the Norfolks' position. Capt Frank Beck the commanding officer of the Sandringham company, looked along the line of his troops. He could call every man by name and had known many of them since they were children. They had always looked to him for leadership and as the moment of attack drew closer and they began to draw on their reserves of energy and courage they looked to him once again. Not far from Beck was private George Carr, just fourteen years old. George was not a regular member of the battalion and had enlisted shortly after the outbreak of the war, having first helped to bring in the all important harvest. He was big for his age and had managed to hoodwink the recruiting sergeant and enlist as a territorial. Capt Beck smiled down at him and winked hoping to renew the boy's courage. Suddenly the silence was shattered by the shrill sounds of a dozen whistles ordering the attack: 'Come on Sandringhams!' Capt Frank Beck, walking-stick in one hand and army issue revolver in the other, climbed out of the trench at the head of his men and began to walk towards the Turkish positions. As the sun beat down on the company and the dust of battle began to swirl around them it must have seemed a very long way from Norfolk and their beloved Sandringham estate.

Robert Reyce, writing about the Norfolk landscape in the seventeenth century described it as being 'void of any great hills, high mountains, or steep rocks; notwithstanding which it is not always so low or flat, but in every place it is severed and divided with little hills easy for ascent and pleasant rivers watering the low valleys'. Certainly a quick look at a map of the county from King's Lynn in the north, to Yarmouth in the south and Norwich at its heart will show that it is not as flat as is usually supposed. However, that said, one of the county's strongest characteristics is its very wide sky. The atmosphere is brilliantly clear, the air sharp and bracing, the winds are cold, keen, and often very strong as they blow almost unchecked from the North pole, twisting coastal trees as they pass. The Norfolk scenery is both varied and beautiful, all around the coastline are wide marshes, many of which are wild and bird-haunted, while others have been drained and cultivated. To the south is the Waveney Valley with its dykes and windmills, many in various stages of decay and collapse, and inland there are rivers and lush water meadows with many willows, oaks and ashes and long hedgerows. Norfolk has not however escaped the effects of man, who has used the landscape in a variety of ways: divided it into square fields for farming, mined it for flint, marl and crag and criss-crossed it with railways, roads, tracks and turnpikes. The gathering of peat created the Norfolk Broads, one of the finest river systems in the country, enjoyed by countless thousands of people over the years. Here you will find rare species of plants, birds, and butterflies; bitterns, grebes, and bearded tits all make their home here and a host of unusual birds pass through on their annual migrations.

There are over 1,300 parishes in Norfolk, their names are like a roll-call of their founders. Many of the towns around the coast were created out of the Victorian craze for sea bathing. The houses in these areas are built of local stone like chalk and brown carrstone, pebble or flint, their roofs are pantiled, sometimes red but more often the typical Norfolk shiny, dark-blue glaze. In contrast the cottages inland are built from clay lump, painted pink or white, with very steeply pitched roofs, usually thatched, and sometimes with black painted weather-boarding. These villages are very picturesque with narrow streets of eighteenth and nineteenth-century houses. Norfolk was once the most densely populated part of Britain with a flourishing foreign trade but over the years it has become, and in many ways remains, a very remote and even a lonely place. Many of the indigenous populations are isolated and keep themselves to themselves and the villages, although close together, remain distinctive and separate. Ploughed fields during the winter and large expanses of golden corn during the summer give away its history, which is that of the development of English agriculture as modern farming techniques turned the county into the 'bread basket of England' and quickly remind people of the rural nature of the area. Medieval and nineteenth century 'wool' churches are everywhere, their church towers dominating the landscape, many are decorated and protected by locally mined flint, making them almost indestructible. The county also boasts artists and poets like Constable and Gainsborough who came for 'the climate and the light' and George Crabb, probably the county's most celebrated poet.

Before the Great War the two great industries of Norfolk were farming and fishing. Before mechanisation farming was hard, menial and tedious, and demanded an army of farm labourers. Steam power applied to the mill, the threshing machine and the plough had reduced some of the need but the farming communities of Norfolk still relied heavily on the horse for ploughing, harrowing, reaping, binding and carting and they continued to do so, well into the twentieth century. The great Shire horses still pulled the ploughs across acres of fields guided by the experienced hands of a ploughman and surrounded by birds. The carts that transported the farmworkers to their place of work and removed stacks of hay to the protection of giant barns were all horse drawn. Villages still had saddle and harness makers, the blacksmith and wheelwright remained two of the most important trades within any district. From Yarmouth the great herring fleets set sail to catch thousands of tons of fish for the local markets and hundreds of nimble fingered women gutted and prepared the fish. It was a slow, gentle world where everyone knew everyone else. Rarely did anyone leave the area and generation after generation was born, lived and died within the same small village community. The concept of travel was unknown, a trip to the local market was all most people attempted or, if they were feeling particularly adventurous, a visit to Norwich, the county's capital, a journey that would probably have taken them several days. The farming communities comprised simple patriotic people who derived, like their poetry and art, their most powerful impulses from the land. It was here in this land and amongst these people that the Royal Family decided to have one of its most important and much-loved homes.

Just over a century ago, Sandringham was a poor parish of just over fifty inhabitants, with a common heath of 200 acres stretching to the village of Wolferton. Sandringham appears in the Domesday book as Sant Dersingham, the name Dersingham being a mixture of Celtic and Anglo-Saxon words meaning 'the dwelling of the water meadow' and 'Sant' meaning 'sand'. Today much of Dersingham, together with many other villages in the surrounding area, forms part of the Royal Estate. We know little of Roger de Sandringham who lived there during the reign of Edward III, and from his hands the land passed to the Cobb family. The estate was then sold to James Hoste who was related to Robert Walpole, the future prime minister and then to the Hon. Charles Spencer Cowper, a step-son of the prime minister, Lord Palmerston. Cowper decided to sell the house and estate to live permanently in France. Although Prince Edward (later King Edward VII) had an official residence in London, Marlborough House, it was decided that, as he would shortly be coming of age, he should have his own home where he could escape, when circumstances allowed, to enjoy the benefits of country living and private relaxation among friends. On 4 February 1862, less than eight weeks after the death of his father Prince Albert, Prince Edward went to view the Sandringham estate. The house he saw was built during the second half of the eighteenth century by Cornish Henley, whose wife's family (Hoste) had owned the property for nearly a hundred years. Henley had demolished the original house and erected in its place a plain but comfortable Georgian one. Among those accompanying the Prince to Sandringham was Sir Charles Phipps, Keeper of the Privy Purse, who sent an enthusiastic report about the estate to Queen Victoria. He wrote: 'The outside of the house was ugly, but it was pleasant and convenient within, and set in pretty grounds. Although the surrounding country was plain, the property was in excellent order, and the opportunity of securing it should not be missed.' He agreed to the purchase and the property was acquired for the price of £220,000.

After having made the house habitable, the Prince left England for a meeting with Princess Alexandra, the daughter of the future King Christian IX and Queen Louise of Denmark, and a few days after the meeting their engagement was announced and the wedding took place at Windsor the following March. At the end of the month Prince Edward brought Princess Alexandra to their new home at Sandringham. Prince Edward and Princess Alexandra loved

1. Sandringham House

the place and spent as much time as possible there. The shooting was good and many of the crowned heads of Europe visited the Royal estate. Prince Edward's hospitality was legendary, he entertained lavishly, and to prove that guests had enjoyed themselves they were weighed upon their arrival and upon their departure; invariably they would have put on a few pounds. Sandringham was also the home of the Royal Stud and many famous racehorses have been trained there, including Persimmon and Diamond Jubilee, both of which later won the Derby. It was soon discovered that the Royal couple would require more room, and both Park House and Batchelor's Cottage were built. In 1893 Prince George (later King George V), who had been created Duke of York, asked for the hand of the Princess Mary, fiancée of his late brother (the Duke of Clarence). She accepted, and they were married in July, spending their honeymoon at Batchelor's Cottage on the Royal estate, (later renamed York Cottage), which eventually became their country home. As their family grew the cottage had to be enlarged twice. All of King George's children, except King Edward VIII, were born there. After the death of Edward VII, King George V continued to live in York Cottage, and it was not until the death of his mother, Queen Alexandra, in 1925 that King George and Queen Mary finally moved into Sandringham House.

Sandringham has always been a working estate and required a large staff to keep it maintained and it has therefore always employed a great number of people from the local area: gardeners, farmers, labourers, gamekeepers, stable hands and household servants. Over the years close bonds have developed between the estate workers and the Royal Family, bonds that are still in evidence today. Family names like Batterbee and Grimes became synonymous with the Royal estate as generation after generation continued to work in and around Sandringham. The Royal Family always took a close interest in the welfare of their workers and knew most of them by name. The Beck family have had a long connection with the Royal estate. Although Prince Edward's first Land Agent was Thomas Henry Burroughes, who served at Sandringham between 1862 and 1865, it was Edmund Beck, who became King Edward VII's land agent in 1865, who was responsible for introducing many of the improvements and modernising the estate. He died tragically as a result of a carriage accident at the gates to York Cottage in 1891 and is commemorated in the church of St Mary Magdalene nearby. After Edmund Beck's death his son Frank followed in his footsteps and became a much-loved and trusted member of the Royal household for the next twenty-five years. The King's agent at Sandringham had not only to be involved in his Royal duties but needed to be an important member of the local community. To this end Frank Beck accepted a commission into the third Volunteer battalion of the Norfolk Regiment and became a member of one of the most famous regiments in the British Army.

Chapter two

The Regiment

The bugles of England
were blowing o'er the sea
As they had called a thousand years,
Calling now to me;
they woke me from dreaming
In the dawning of the day,
The bugles of England ...
And how could I stay?

James Drummond Burns (1823-1864)

The Royal Norfolk Regiment one of the oldest and most distinguished regiments in the British Army. It has its own chapel in Norwich Cathedral, the walls of which are lined with flags. Embroidered into their decaying cloth are over three hundred years of battle honours, sacrifice and service to the Crown. It is a fitting tribute to the thousands of Norfolk people who over the years have made the supreme sacrifice for their country.

The Norfolk regiment can trace its ancestry back to 1685 when it was raised to help combat the Duke of Monmouth's rebellion against James II. The King raised eight new infantry regiments, numbering them 8 to 15, one of these being Colonel Henry Cornwall's Regiment of Foot, later to be known as the 9th Foot and eventually the Royal Norfolk Regiment. Although they were not used against the Duke of Monmouth, who was eventually defeated at Sedgmoor and later executed, they were used in 1687 to quell serious rioting which had broken out in York. During these disturbances, the regiment's Commanding Officer, Lieutenant-Colonel Purcell, earned an infamous reputation for sentencing civilian rioters to inhuman military punishments.

Between 1689 and 1691 the regiment was sent to Ireland to intervene in a civil war heavy with religious fervour between James II, who drew his support from the Catholic South and William of Orange, whose strength lay in the protestant North, a situation not unfamiliar today, where the regiment is still serving, still trying to preserve the peace. During the Irish campaign the regiment were engaged against James II's forces at the Battle of the Boyne and Aughrim as well as taking an important part in the sieges of Limerick and Athlone. The campaign is still celebrated in Northern Island today with a public holiday and marches. With the fall of Limerick the 'Irish War' was finally brought to a conclusion, although, unfortunately for the Norfolks, they had to remain behind for several more years on garrison duty.

In 1694 the Norfolks took part in the disastrous landing against the French at Brest. The Duke of Marlborough, badly out of favour with William III, having discovered the details of the landings passed on this information to James II, who in turn informed his friend Louis XIV of France and thus gave the French over a month to prepare their defences against the British assault. After landing the 9th made a frontal assault against the French, who were securely entrenched and had strong support from their artillery, and the attacking force were quite literally cut to pieces. In this assault almost a thousand British troops lost their lives, including the Commanding Officer General Talmash, who knew he had been a victim of treachery.

The regiment next became involved in the War of the Spanish Succession, a war which was to drag on for eleven years, the first six of which involved the 9th in almost continuous fighting. They were present at the storming of Venloo in 1702 and in 1704 were sent to Portugal to help stiffen the Portuguese resolve against the common enemy, Spain and France. While in Portugal the regiment was to suffer one of its many disasters when, under the command of Lieutenant-Colonel Hussey, they were besieged in the small fortress of Castello de Vide and due to the treachery of the Portuguese, who destroyed their powder by throwing it down a well, the entire regiment was forced to surrender and were marched into captivity in France.

Fortunately the regiment were not prisoners long and were released later that year as part of a prisoner exchange following the Duke of Marlborough's overwhelming victory at the battle of Blenheim. After a vigorous recruiting campaign the Norfolks were quickly brought up to strength and they later took part in the battle of Alcantara and Almanza, where they distinguished themselves and more than made up for their earlier disgrace. Unfortunately after the latter action the regiment's casualties were so high that it almost ceased to exist and on its return to England in 1708 the regiment could barely muster one hundred men.

The next fifty-four years were relatively peaceful for the regiment, then in 1761 they were again in action, this time taking part in the landing on Belle Isle, a French colony lying off Quiberon Bay in the Bay of Biscay. After the French capitulation the 9th remained to garrison the island until 1762, when they were involved in an attack against the Spanish possession of Cuba. Although the British won an overwhelming victory, their ranks were terribly depleted by disease, which swept through the regiment, more men dying of fever than as a result of enemy action.

In 1775, after numerous political blunders by the British government and King George III, the American colonies went to war with Britain. In April 1776, the 9th regiment sailed from Cork to Quebec to take part in the struggle for America. Despite the campaign being a series of disasters for Britain, the chief architect of which was the Secretary of State for the Colonies, Lord George Sackville, the Norfolks were to distinguish themselves. They first saw action on 8 June 1776, when they were part of a force attacked by superior numbers of American troops at the Three Rivers. As the Americans advanced in a frontal assault they were shot down by the disciplined volleys of the British infantrymen and suffered heavy casualties. The 9th then became part of General 'Gentleman Johnny' Burgoyne's force, which was to form part of a three-pronged advance against the American forces.

Burgoyne was to advance from Canada southwards by Ticonderoga to the Hudson at Saratoga, and then on to Albany. The British were between 7,000 and 8,000 strong, including 250 artillerymen and 500 Indians. On paper they were a powerful force. Despite this, however, they advanced into complete disaster. The 9th took part in several notable battles. At South Bay, although outnumbered two to one, they beat off the attacking American force. At Fort St Anne they stood firm against an American army six times their number, finally repulsing them. Unfortunately the British were slowly undermined and their force was whittled down to less than 4,000 men and these were half starved, low on ammunition and surrounded by 16,000 Americans. On 16 October 1777 Burgoyne was forced to surrender at Saratoga. It was one of the darkest days in British military history and for the next three years the 9th foot would spend their time as prisoners-of-war. In 1781 the remnants of the regiment returned to England, where Lieutenant-Colonel Hill presented to the King the regimental colours he had managed to conceal in his baggage at the time of their surrender at Saratoga.

In 1782 while the regiment was quartered in Norwich, the King decreed that it should: 'take the county name of 9th or East Norfolk Regiment ... so as to create a mutual attachment between the county and the regiment which may at all times be useful towards recruiting the regiment'.

In 1797 a year notable for reforms within the British Army (with pay increasing to a shilling a day), the Norfolks began to look more like the county's regiment. Over the next few years they were stationed at Bury St Edmunds, Colchester, Yarmouth, Sudbury, Clacton, Ipswich and Stowmarket. In 1799 the King gave them the privilege of bearing the figure of Britannia as the regimental badge.

The regiment was next to take a prominent part in the grossly mismanaged campaign in Holland. Losses on both sides were high, with the Norfolks losing over 350 men. The end of the campaign in Holland and the signing of the Peace of Amiens saw a peaceful respite for the regiment. However, even during this period of calm the regiment was to suffer. On 10 November 1805 the regiment set sail from Cork for England on board the transport ships *Jane*, *Harriett* and *Ariadne*. When they reached the Straits of Dover they encountered bad weather, and although the *Jane* and the *Harriett* managed to struggle to port, the *Ariadne* was forced onto the French coast and wrecked. The regiment not only lost all its baggage, records and plate but Colonel de Berniere and the entire Regimental Headquarters staff of 262 men were taken prisoner by the French.

The 9th was next involved in the Peninsula War, winning no less than nine battle honours: Rolica, Vimiera, Corunna, Busaco, Salamanca, Vittoria, St Sebastian, Nive and the Peninsula, as they pushed Napoleon's army out of Spain. At Rolica the 29th Foot (Worcestershire) Regiment were suffering badly having lost their colours and over 200 men and were in danger of being overwhelmed and annihilated by a large French force. Lieutenant-Colonel Stuart, commanding the 9th, ordered the regiment to fix bayonets and attack the French. The Norfolks advanced against them 'perfectly dressed' as if on a ceremonial parade and totally routed the French. Their timely arrival saved the 29th Foot from certain disaster, and allowed them to recover their colours despite desperate counter attacks. At Vimiera the regiment was in reserve and won its battle honour a little more easily.

By 1808 Napoleon had over 130,000 troops under arms in Spain. Sir John Moore, now in command of the British army, had 40,000 men under his command, the 9th being in the Brigade commanded by General Beresford. As Moore and his army made their way towards Salamanca he learned of the disastrous defeat of the Spanish Army by the French and that Napoleon was marching towards Madrid with overwhelming forces determined to drive the British into the sea. Moore, realising the gravity of the situation, turned his troops north-west in an attempt to re-embark his army at Corunna. After a long and exhausting march the British army arrived at Corunna to find that the British fleet had been delayed by bad weather, so the army turned to face Marshal Soult, one of Napoleon's greatest generals. The French threw themselves against the British time and time again but Moore's army stood firm. The 9th formed part of the rear guard as the ships arrived and the troops began to embark. Unfortunately at the moment of victory Sir John Moore was shot and killed. He was carried from the field by men of the 9th regiment and buried by them in his marshall's cloak. The 9th were the very last regiment to leave the shores of Spain, Captain Gomm claiming the distinction of being the last man to embark. Despite their glorious stand at Corunna casualties had been high and the 9th had been virtually wiped out once again.

The 9th returned to Spain in 1810 and took part in the battle of Busaco in September where their bayonet charge finally drove the French from the heights and won the day, as it had some years before at Rolica. They were then heavily engaged at the battle of Salamanca, the most decisive and bloody battle of the Peninsula Campaign. When Colonel Cameron, known to his men as, 'The Devil' and then in command of the 9th, heard the order to advance he replied, 'Thank you sir, that's the best news I've had today.' He commanded his men, 'Now boys, we'll at them!'. The regiment went on to distinguish itself at the battles of Vittoria, St Sebastian and the Nive. After the Peninsula, the 9th was stationed in Canada before returning to form part of the army of occupation in France following Napoleon's final defeat at Waterloo. In September 1835, after a period in the West Indies where sickness once again took a terrible toll amongst the regiment, the 9th were sent to India for the first time, beginning a relationship with the continent that was to last for over a century. The regiment was to play a full part in the long and bloody history of British rule in India.

Their first taste of the constant wars that almost ceaselessly ravaged India came after the destruction of the British Army under General Elphinstone as he tried to retreat from Afghanistan. The 9th were commanded to force the infamous Khyber Pass, which they did at the point of a bayonet, marching into Kabul despite suffering over a hundred casualties on their way. On their return from Kabul the 9th became involved in the First Sikh War of 1845. The Sikhs were led by Ranjit Singh and were trained and armed by Europeans, with over 300 field guns, 35,000 infantry and 15,000 cavalry. Sir Hugh Gough, the British commander, was able to muster only 31,000 men, barely a quarter of which were British. He was also out-gunned by the Sikhs who were equipped with some of the latest European built cannon, many of them of a large calibre. At Ferozeshah the British attacked a strongly held Sikh position. They advanced over open ground with little cover, while shot and shell rained down on them. Not surprisingly, they were stopped in their tracks and forced back. The following day the British attacked again, and once again cut to ribbons by the Sikh guns but this time, despite being out-numbered three to one, pressed on. The bayonet finally decided the outcome and the Sikhs fled the battle field leaving much of their equipment and guns behind. The British captured seventy-two guns but suffered over 2,000 casualties, the 9th alone suffered almost 300 casualties. The Sikh army are believed to have suffered over 5,000 men killed and wounded.

The final battle of the First Sikh War was at Sobraon; though the 9th were in reserve they did take part in the final charge which routed the Sikh army. The regiment were awarded the battle honours Kabul, Moodkee, Ferozeshah and Sobraon. The bravery and determination of the 9th would be long remembered in India.

In March 1854, England declared war on Russia. The 9th were soon landed near Balaclava, the advance base for the British Army besieging Sebastopol, before being quickly moved into the front-line trenches. Life in the trenches before Sebastopol was grim. Clothing, food, shelter, fuel and medicines were all in short supply, 8,000 men of the original expeditionary force were already in makeshift hospitals, and the death rate among those admitted exceeded 88 per cent. Four men died from disease to every one killed by enemy action. Within a week of landing the 9th had lost fifty-seven soldiers to disease and by the end of 1854 that number had risen to over one hundred. On 8 September 1855, the key positions in the defence of Sebastopol, the Malakoff and the Redan, were finally captured by a combined attack by the British and French. The following day the Russians set the town on fire, sank their fleet and retreated across the River Tchernaya and the war was over. The peace treaty was signed in Paris on 30 March 1856. Between November 1854, when the regiment landed in Russia, and April 1856, when they finally departed, the 9th suffered 108 casualties as a result of enemy action while almost double that number succumbed to sickness or died of disease.

In 1857 the 9th became a two-battalion regiment. Over the next few years they were to be stationed at various places throughout England and the world, taking part in several 'little wars' as Britain expanded and maintained its mighty Empire. They saw action during the Second Afghan War in 1879 and fought in the jungles of Burma against the Chins. In January 1900 twenty-six officers and 984 men set sail on the Assaye to take part in the South African War against the rebellious Boer farmers. The war was not going well for the British and they had suffered heavy losses at the hands of a very mobile and determined enemy. With the arrival of Lord Roberts and his Chief of Staff Lord Kitchener the situation began to change and the British began to get the upper hand. Although not heavily engaged in the campaign, places like Paardeberg, Vanderberg Drift and Kimberley would be long remembered by the men of the Norfolk Regiment.

The next few years saw the British Army spending much of its time consolidating its hard won Empire; then in 1914 came a disaster that was to shake the very foundations of European society. By its sheer scale the First World War dwarfed all other wars, causing more casualties than all the old colonial campaigns put together, and tearing the very heart out of the British, and their Empire.

The British Expeditionary Force crossed to France between 7 and 10 August 1914. The 1st Norfolks reached Le Havre where they were warmly welcomed by the local population and on 17

2. *Officers and NCOs of the Sandringham Company:* (Left to right) *Sergeant S.A. Lines, Sergeant E.W. Crosbie, Sergeant T.H. Cook, (head gardener), Captain F.R. Beck, Sergeant F. Sharpe, Captain A. Knight, Sergeant F.W. Bland, (head gamekeeper), Company Sergeant-Major H.L. Saward (Beck Collection).*

August they entrained for the front. The Norfolks formed part of Major General Sir Charles Ferguson's 5th Division and it was in saving this division that they took part in one of the greatest rearguard actions in history. On arrival at the front, the Norfolks dug themselves in along the Mons-Condé canal and awaited the German attack; it was not long in coming. At dawn on 24 August 1914, the full force of the German war machine fell upon Ferguson's division. Despite showing great gallantry and killing the enemy in their hundreds the division was forced to retire. The Germans followed up their attack and the pressure was great. If what was left of the division was to get out intact a rearguard action would have to be fought to protect its uncovered left flank. Only two battalions could be spared for the action and the job was entrusted to the 1st Norfolks and the 1st Cheshires, with Lieutenant-Colonel Charles Ballard commanding. They were opposed by the whole 4th German Army Corps, consisting of twenty-five battalions of infantry, six squadrons of cavalry, twenty-four batteries of artillery and fifty-six machine guns. As the 5th Division began to pull out, the Germans launched their attack. The Norfolks did not even have time to entrench but had to take cover in the open countryside. They stopped the German attacks again and again but still they came on and both the Norfolks and the Cheshires were becoming dangerously isolated. Colonel Ballard, seeing that most of the 5th Division had retired, gave the order to pull back. 'It's time to go,' he told his Adjutant, Capt Cresswell, 'Get a message to the Cheshires telling them to retire after us.' Runners were sent to warn the Cheshires but they were all killed, including Capt Cresswell. Colonel Bogor, commanding the Cheshires fought on, obeying his last order telling him to hold his position to the last man and the last round. The Norfolks managed to reach the rest of the brigade, but the Cheshires were surrounded and despite the greatest gallantry wiped out. The stand of the Norfolks and the Cheshires had saved the 5th division. The Norfolks, now part of General Smith-Dorrien's 2nd corps, fell back on Le Cateau from where, after a brief stand against the oncoming Germans, they continued to retreat. They marched almost non-stop for seven days, covering over 200 miles, and were pushed back almost to the gates of Paris itself. It had been one of the greatest fighting retreats in military history.

Meanwhile the 2nd battalion, who had been in India, were sent to Mesopotamia, forming part of the 18th Indian brigade. They were to spend most of their war fighting the Turks, an enemy they soon learnt to respect. At Shaiba on 14 April 1915, Colonel Peebles and the rest of the officers of the 2nd battalion went into action against the Turks carrying their swords – the last occasion in the British Army that officers were to carry swords in action.

As it became clear that the war would not be 'all over by Christmas', men poured into the recruiting offices in Norfolk answering the call to serve King and Country. Lord Kitchener's pointing finger and belligerent moustache had done their job well. Men in their twenties and thirties, middle-aged men and even under-age boys all queued up to take the King's shilling and enlist before it was all over. They came from as far afield as Yarmouth and King's Lynn, from little villages like Overstrand, Cley-next-the-sea, Melton Constable and Honing. Within six months of Britain declaring war on Germany the two battalions of the Norfolk regiment had become nine. And then there were the two territorial battalions who had trained for years for just such an occasion. Now it was time for them to prove their worth.

The territorial battalions owed their existence to the establishment of the Volunteer Force in 1859. The force was formed to help allay the Victorian fear of a French invasion of Britain. After initial reservations, the volunteer companies became very popular and by 1860 it is estimated that the force was approximately 119,000 strong. It was the Boer War at the turn of the century and the consequent searching examination into the British Army that followed that finally saw an end to the volunteers and to the establishment of the Territorial Army. The Boer War had affected the volunteers in three ways. By serving overseas it raised questions of their efficiency and the likelihood of them serving overseas again (over 30,000 volunteers served with the British army during the Boer War). It became clear that with the regular army serving abroad the public did not have complete faith in the volunteer corps to defend the country against invasion and finally the volunteers became part of the general debate about the army which was to last until 1914.

On the 4 March 1907 Haldane introduced his Territorial and Reserve Forces Bill into the House of Commons. In the Autumn of 1907, the Lords Lieutenant were encouraged to establish County Associations to run the new force. The climax of all this effort came on 26 October 1907, when King Edward VII invited all the Lords Lieutenant to Buckingham Palace. In this way he firmly identified himself with the new force. Haldane was later to comment, 'The King's intervention has produced the requisite steam for the engine, and I am working day and night to take full advantage of the moment.'

However despite all Haldane's hard work this still did not satisfy everybody and the Norwich council was far from unanimous in its approval of the formation of the new force. In 1908 Councillor Louis Tillett sent the following letter to the Secretary for War.

> Dear Mr Haldane,
>
> At a meeting of the City Council the other day the very important question of giving facilities to the corporation employees who wish to join the Territorial Force was under consideration. We have five socialist gentlemen in the council, and they objected strongly to facilities being given on the ground that the local Territorial Force could be ordered away to various parts of the country to suppress disturbances arising from labour disputes. Will you kindly send me a line, saying whether the local force would be liable to such orders either in time of peace or after mobilisation.
>
> I'm sorry to trouble you with this line but the point raised is important to us here.

Haldane replied four days later.

> Dear Mr Tillet,
>
> The local Territorial Force can not be embodied for the purpose of putting down disturbances arising from labour disputes either in their own locality or at a distance. By the law of this country if there is a riot, and a danger to life or violent destruction of property is about to be committed, every citizen may be called into aid and a Territorial soldier no less than any other.
>
> But we were careful when the act passed through parliament, to leave out all provisions enabling the force to be embodied for this purpose in the fashion in which the regular soldier might be, of course, if the force had been embodied for some other legitimate reason, say mobilization on the outbreak of war, and there were a riot, its members might be called on to help like any other person …

Having reassured everybody Haldane went on to take advantage of the situation. Despite the regular army looking down on these part time 'Saturday Night' soldiers, by 1909 no fewer than 115 members of the House of Lords were serving on County Associations. In 1910 members of the Territorial Force were asked to volunteer for duty overseas, and by January 1913 1,152 officers and 18,903 NCOs and other ranks were under engagement to serve abroad on mobilization. By 1912 there were fifty-seven Conservative and thirty-seven Liberal MPs serving with the Territorial Forces. In Norfolk the 3rd Volunteer Battalion and the Norfolk Regiment amalgamated with the 2nd Volunteer Battalion to form the 5th Territorial Battalion the Norfolk Regiment which formed part of the East Anglian Division consisting of the 4th and 5th battalions of the Norfolk Regiment, the 1st East Anglian Field Artillery Brigade, the 6th Cyclist battalion of the Norfolk Regiment, the first East Anglian Field Ambulance and a company of the Army Service Corps.

Of the Territorial Army's service during the First World War Sir John French was to comment: 'I say without the slightest hesitation that without the assistance that the Territorials afforded it would have been impossible to have held the line in France and Belgium and have prevented the enemy from reaching the Channel sea ports.'

The Territorials had at last come of age.

Chapter three

The Battalion

Youth in its flush and flower
Has a soul of whitest flame,
Eternity in an hour,
All life and death in a game.

Noel Hodgson
Killed in Action on the Somme 1 July 1916

Having shown his support for the founding of the new Territorial Force, King Edward VII decided to take a more practical part in its formation by raising a company from his country estate at Sandringham and enlisting them into one of the newly formed local territorial battalions. During a visit to Sandringham in 1908 King Edward approached his land agent Frank Beck, and asked him to form a company of men exclusively from workers on the estate and surrounding area. Although Beck already held the rank of captain in the local Volunteer Force, and a number of other workers on the estate helped to make up the rank and file, but there were by no means enough of them to form a company. Capt Beck set about his task with a vengeance and quickly raised over a hundred men, all of them estate workers, and enlisted them into the 5th Territorial Battalion of the Norfolk Regiment, where they became 'E' company.

The 5th Norfolks were made up of eight companies, each of which consisted of around a hundred officers and men. Although a few came from outside, most of them were Norfolk men and all parts of the county were represented. The allocation of men to each company depended largely upon in which part of the county they lived or worked, which suited most recruits who were more than happy to serve with their friends and aquaintances.

'A' company came from in and around the King's Lynn area and became known as the 'Lynn Company'. The pattern continued, 'B' was from Downham, 'C' from Fakenham (with detachments in Aylsham and Wells), 'D' from Dereham (with a detachment at

3. Dereham Company route march 1915.

Swaffham), 'E' from Sandringham, 'F' from Cromer (with detachments at Sheringham, Holt, and Melton Constable), 'G' from Gt Yarmouth and 'H' from North Walsham (with a detachment from Gt Yarmouth).

In October 1909, during a Royal visit to Norfolk, King Edward VII presented colours to the newly formed territorial battalions, including the 5th Battalion, after which they formed up and marched past their King. Many of the territorials looked on their service as a bit of a lark, an excuse to make a bit of extra money and get away from the wife or a mundane job for a short while. They drilled several times a week and each village and town had its own drill hall for this purpose. There were inter-company and inter-battalion sports like football, cricket, athletics and rifle shooting. Private Tom Williamson remembers winning the rifle shooting competitions on both the indoor and outside ranges, and after the annual dinner when he was presented with two cups and two medals for his achievement he was carried shoulder high around Cromer with a military band in full regalia playing a popular march. Once or sometimes twice a year they attended an annual camp which lasted anything from one to two weeks, where they would practise manoeuvres and battle-field tactics both during the day and at night. The camps were never too far from home; the Sandringham's annual camp was held at Wolferton, a small village just outside Sandringham, convenient if any of the workers were required urgently back on the estate. Despite their amateur appearance however, by the outbreak of the First War they had become a determined and capable fighting force and were to take an important part in the fighting.

The battalion was a very close-knit society, made up as it was of relatives, friends, neighbours and work mates. Its rank structure reflected the society of the time: the local gentry and land-owners formed the officer corps, the foremen, head gardeners and game keepers became the NCOs and the rank and file were made up of farm hands, gardeners, labourers and household servants. The battalion's commanding officer was Lieutenant-Colonel Sir Horace George Proctor-Beauchamp CB (6th Bart) of Langly Hall, who had taken over command on 11 November 1914, replacing Colonel Thomas. Sir Horace was born on 3 November 1856 and entered the army in 1878. He served with his regiment, the 20th Hussars, during the Sudan expeditions between 1885-1886, where he was mentioned in despatches for his bravery. He then travelled to India and took part in a number of skirmishes and small wars. He next saw action during the Boer War and was again mentioned in

4. Lynn Company, King's Lynn market square 1914.

5. The Sandringham Company at Wolferton Camp 19 June 1912:

Back Row left to Right: *G. Batterbee, R. Ringer, E. Watts, B. Borley, G.R. Dove, H. Harlow, A. Ford, W. Finch, E. Emmerson, G.H. Batterbee, V. Wells, G. Wells, A. Watts, E. Hudson, C. Hunter, R. Bridges.*

Second Row: *W.H. Yaxley, G. Daniels, Hunt, F. Melton, J. Dye, B. Reynolds, A. Batterbee, J. Nurse, J. Batterbee, W. Goodman, W. Bridges, G. Deaves, W. Jakeman, A. Bridges, A. Emmerson, P. Smith, P. Loose, A. Waters, F. Wells, H. Lindford, S. Goodship, W. Humphrey, W. Grimes, W. Ringer, H. Elworth, C. Beckett, H. Garney.*

Third Row: *G. Melton, W. Grapes, S.A. Lines, G.R. Primrose, F.P. Sharpe, F.W. Bland (head keeper), T.H. Cook (head gardener), E.W. Crosbie, J.V. Betts, Capt F.R. Beck, Coln. Petre (former commanding officer), Rev A.R.H. Grant (rector of Sandringham), Capt A. Knight, H.L. Saward, R. Crome, Lieut. G. Riches, H. Bugg, R. Barrell.*

Fourth Row: *F. Cross, W. Standaloft, W. Cross, B. Grimes, F. Patrick, A. Daniels, P. Daw, A. Grimes, G. Playford, W. Mindham, T. Houehen, A. Nurse, H. Wasey, D. Godfrey, C. Grimes, P. Hammond, H. Dawes, E. Bunting, H. Todd, E. Bland.*

Fifth Row: *J. Woods, J. Crome, E. Steele, J. Hanslip, L. Curson, R. Mussett, O. Carter, W. Hipkin, H. Willmott, A.W. Nurse, J. Hudson, F. Woodhouse, G. Needs, J.W. Godfray, E. Cox, F. Woodward, R. Overman.*

Sixth Row: *F.R. Kerriston, E. Melton, H. Merrikin, D. Howell, C. Howell, F. Turley, S. Carter, A. Bridges, S. Smith, C. Basham.*

despatches for his courage. He was made a CB in 1902 before retiring from the army in 1904. He was re-commissioned in 1914, largely because of a shortage of experienced officers to command an ever-expanding army. Sir Horace was popular with his men, one of whom later wrote of him,

> Two or three times a week parades were held and each night the commandant was at his post dominating the proceedings by a combination of geniality and strictness which mark the

6. Lieutenant-Colonel Sir Horace Proctor-Beachamp.

> leader apart from the led. I can see him now, watching us from different parts of the Town Hall while we practised with the rudiments of squad drill, or stalking about the room with stick and eye glass. The new training was not what he had been accustomed to – he admitted as much; the 20th Hussars which he used to command, knew little if anything, of platoons and infantry formations. We learnt to lean on him heavily, he drew the best out of us and we trusted him to put things right if anything went wrong. Thus that painful sense of futility which a civilian corps would naturally feel in trying to master the art of discipline so strange to their upbringing gradually left us. No one could have been more inspiring, yet no one would have kept us more alive to the seriousness of what we were attempting. Those who met Sir Horace privately soon learned the secret of his success for religion was of the utmost reality to him and it was personal worth that gave him his remarkable ascendancy over the men who came under his sway.

As if to illustrate the strong family ties within the battalion Sir Horace's nephew, Second-Lieutenant Montague Barclay Granville Proctor-Beauchamp, also served with it. He had joined the battalion, so he said, to 'keep an eye on his uncle'. Montague was young, energetic, very popular with his men, and the life and soul of any party.

Capt Frank Beck had also brought his two nephews with him, Albert Edward Alexander, known as Alec, and Arthur Evelyn, who preferred to be known as Evelyn. To try to prevent confusion they became known as Black (Frank), White (Alec), and Pink (Evelyn) Beck. Frank Beck had been born on 3 May 1861 at Oxwick in Norfolk, the third of six children of Edmund and Anna Maria Beck. Frank's father was a farmer, land agent and auctioneer before being appointed in 1865 land agent to the then Prince of Wales, later King Edward VII. Frank was educated at the Norfolk County School at North Elmham where he became school captain. In 1880 he joined his father as assistant in the estate office at Sandringham. He hunted, raced point-to-point and assisted Lord Marcus Beresford, His Royal Highness' racing manager, in the management of the thoroughbred stud at Sandringham. In 1891 he married a local girl, Mary Plumpton Wilson of West Newton, and they had six children, five daughters and a son (tragically, the son died in infancy). In 1891, Frank's father died suddenly after a coach

7. Second-Lieutenant Montague Barclay Granville Proctor-Beachamp.

accident at the gates to York Cottage on the Sandringham estate and at the age of thirty Frank took over his duties as agent to the Prince of Wales. He also worked closely with General Sir Dighton Probyn, Comptroller and Treasurer to the Prince's Household and later Keeper of the Privy Purse to King Edward VII. During this time the General and Frank became firm friends. As well as his general duties around the estate Frank also attended Tzar Nicholas of Russia when he visited Sandringham in 1894 and Kaiser Wilhelm during a number of visits he made to the Royal estate, later declining a decoration offered to him by the Kaiser. In 1901, with the Prince of Wales's accession to the throne, he was created a

8. Albert Edward Alexander (Alec) Beck.

Member of the Royal Victorian Order (4th class) in the coronation honours. In 1906 he was appointed a Knight of the Order of St Olaf by King Haakon of Norway, who had married King Edward VII's daughter, Princess Maud. After King Edward's death in 1910 he continued as land agent to King George V.

In 1914 Capt Beck almost gave up the military life. After the battalion's annual camp he returned home, threw his jacket onto a chair and said, 'I don't think I'm much of a soldier, I think I'll be done with this now.' A week or two later at the outbreak of the First World War, Capt Beck, although not obliged to go with his company due to his age, was insistent, saying, 'I formed them how could I leave them now? The lads will expect me to go with them, besides I promised their wives and children I would look after them.'

His nephew Alec was born in 1881 on the Sandringham estate, the eldest of seven sons. His father (Frank Beck's brother) also worked as an assistant in the estate office. Later the family moved after his father was appointed land agent on Lord Hasting's estate at Melton Constable, where Alec's brother Evelyn Beck was born. In 1898, Alec was commissioned into the Suffolk Regiment and saw service during the Boer War. On his return he trained as a land agent before being appointed by Sir Oswald Moseley to administer his Rolleston Estate in Staffordshire. He married in 1905 and had five children. Evelyn Beck became a farmer and farmed at both Mintly near King's Lynn and East Tuddenham outside Norwich. The brothers kept in close touch with their uncle and enlisted in the battalion together, Alec also bringing with him Second-Lieutenant Robert Adams, a friend from the Moseley estate. It was the ideal way of getting to spend time together as a family.

The Cubitts of Honing Hall, in the village of Honing in central Norfolk, were also strongly represented within the battalion. There were three brothers, Edward (better known as Randall), Victor and Eustace, as well as their cousin Randall Burroughes and Randall Cubitt's brother-in-law Rolland Pelly. As if that were not enough to add to the inter-relationships the Cubitts were also distantly related to the Proctor-Beauchamps. Randall Cubitt, the heir to the Honing estate, was born in London in 1884 and educated at Repton in Derbyshire, where he was a first-class athlete and made a special study of estate management and the encouragement of English agriculture. On his return to the Honing estate in Norfolk he established a fruit farm, which became the main preoccupation of his life. In October 1913 he married Jane Catherine Pelly, the daughter of Canon R.A. Pelly, the vicar of West Ham, London. Randall Cubitt's Christianity was important to him and when the view of the local parish church from Honing Hall was blocked by a line of trees, he cut an oval shape out of the branches so he could continue to see it. That view remains to this day, and is just as impressive. Although he had held a commission in the 5th Norfolks for some years, he resigned shortly after his marriage to concentrate on his fruit farm, but at the outbreak of hostilities he was immediately re-commissioned into the battalion. His brother,

9. *The Cubitt family:* (left to right) *Lieutenant Victor Cubitt, Second-Lieutenant Randall Burroughes (cousin), Captain Randall Cubbit, Mildred Cubitt (sister), Lieutenant Eustace Cubitt.*

Lieutenant Victor Murray Cubbitt, was born three years after Randall in 1887 and was also educated at Repton. While there he became a keen student of sociology and politics and in 1909 was appointed Organising Secretary of the County Protest League against the budget of that year and received a presentation of plate from the Right Hon. Walter Long in recognition of his services. For some years he acted as Secretary to the Scottish Branch of the Land Agents' Society, having adopted that profession and holding a post on some considerable Scottish estates. At the outbreak of war he hurried back to Honing and received a commission into the battalion. Eustace Henry Cubitt was born in 1889 and maintained the family tradition by also being educated at Repton. After leaving school, he travelled to Ireland and began to farm until the outbreak of the war, when he joined his two brothers.

Their cousin second Lieutenant Randall Burroughes was born in

1896 and educated at Winchester College. He seemed hardly old enough to become a soldier but he too joined the battalion in August 1914 to be close to his relatives (Randall Burroughes was also related to Thomas Henry Burroughes, King Edward VII's first agent at Sandringham, 1863/65). Second-Lieutenant Rolland Pelly, Randall's brother-in-law, also joined to be close to his newly found family.

Also among the officers' ranks were the brothers Marcus and Trevor Oliphant, the sons of the Reverend Francis George Oliphant, rector of Gunthorpe-cum-Bale. They were both educated at Rugby School, after which Marcus obtained a place at Pembroke College, Oxford and Trevor at Exeter College, Oxford. Both men were enthusiastic members of the University's Officer Training Corps. After graduating Marcus became an assistant master at Stanmore School and in 1915 he enlisted into the ranks of the Artists Rifles (28th battalion of the London Regiment) wishing to 'go through the mill' before obtaining a commission. However in April 1915 he was commissioned into the 5th Norfolks, thereby joining his brother and becoming an officer in 'C' company.

Arthur Humfrey Mason was the second son of R.H. Mason, J.P. and was born at Necton Hall, Norfolk in 1883 (alas now demolished and turned into a piggery). He was educated at Charterhouse after which he became a director of Morgan's brewery in Norwich and spent his spare time assisting at the Church of England's Men's Society and in other philanthropic works. He was the brother-in-Law of Capt Arthur Edward Martyr Ward, the battalion's Adjutant. Ward was a regular officer officially belonging to the 1st battalion of the Norfolk Regiment but had been attached to the 5th battalion since 1912. He never missed an opportunity to make it quite clear that he was not too happy about serving with a bunch of 'part-time amateurs' and few missed the rough edge of his tongue. He was however the most experienced and efficient officer the battalion had.

Capt Edmund Gay was born in India in 1883, the son of Edward Gay Esq., who was Comptroller and Auditor General to the government of India. The family returned to England and took up residence at Aldborough Hall, in Norfolk. Capt Gay was educated at the Dragon School, Oxford, where he was remembered as not being too keen on school work but a first class 'slogger' at cricket. From the Dragon School he went to Winchester College, then

New College, Oxford, where he won the lightweights' and novices' boxing competitions. After university he travelled to Ceylon where he spent the next five years tea planting. He returned to Norfolk in 1909 and began to try his hand at farming. He accepted a commission into the battalion at the outbreak of the war in August 1914.

The list of the county's 'brightest and best' continues: Major Woodwark was a prominent local solicitor, in the firm of Sadler and Woodwark in King's Lynn, as well as being the vice-consul for Russia. He had two brothers, both of whom served at one time or the other with the Norfolks. Capt Coxon was a dentist in King's Lynn; Capt Arthur Devereux Pattrick, the commanding officer of the Lynn company, was a partner in the firm of Pattrick and Thompson Ltd, timber merchants. He was commissioned into the volunteers in 1906 and trained with the Grenadier Guards at Chelsea Barracks, where he qualified for his captaincy. He became the commanding officer of the Lynns in February 1914. Major

***10.** Captain Edmund Gay.*

11. Captain Arthur Devereux Pattrick.

Purdy eventually became the second-in-command of the battalion, a very intelligent and literate man and highly respected by his men, of whom it was said they would follow him to hell and back if he ordered it.

The ties amongst the rank and file were no less strong, with families, friends and workmates joining en masse. Towns, villages, and hamlets took a pride in how many men joined up: Castleacre contributed 132 men to the colours, King's Lynn 339. Associations, clubs and firms also took a pride in how many of their men enlisted. Most of the King's Lynn football club enlisted as well as several other members of local football teams, and became very important to the 5th Norfolks in their inter-battalion games, which accounted for their great success. A large number of men from the Midland and Great Northern Joint Railway enlisted together: Station masters, platform attendants, signal operators, clerks, electricians and labourers. Included amongst these was Private Tom Williamson, who had been with the battalion for some years, having been talked into joining by his foreman, who was a company sergeant-major with the battalion. Thomas Williamson was born on 7 June 1894 at Melton Constable, one of thirteen children; his father was an inspector on the Midland and Great Northern joint railway. Tom was educated at the local village school, leaving when he was fourteen years old to become a bricklayer's mate. His father finally got him an apprenticeship as a coach builder with the railway, an apprenticeship that should have lasted five years. He only managed to complete four before his work was interrupted by the outbreak of the war. He joined the territorials in Melton Constable where they had their own drill hall and became a member of 'F' company.

Local school teachers, like nineteen year old Private Frank Rogers, who taught at St James boys' school, were determined to set an example to the boys, old and new. They enlisted into the ranks and served alongside a number of the school's former pupils. There were three members of the Meggitt family from King's Lynn, three members of the Thomson family from Dereham, three members of the Herring family from Hunstanton and three members of the Robinson family from Cromer. From the Royal Estate at Sandringham the roll call showed that several members of the Batterbee family had enlisted as well as the Bridges, the Grimes and the Nurses. Many of these names were well known on the estate and had worked at Sandringham from generation to generation. This sudden loss of man power left Norfolk very short of labour, and women filled many of the roles that would not have been considered fit for the 'gentle sex' prior to the war.

Although it was good for recruiting for men to be able to enlist, train and go to war with people they knew and were familiar with, it also had its dangers. For if the going got tough it almost certainly meant they would die together, thus possibly removing from an area all of its able-bodied men. As most of the agricultural work at that time was labour intensive, the loss of so many men could quite easily destroy a community. But in the euphoria of August 1914 that was the last thing on their minds.

Chapter four

Goodbye-ee

God Knows – my dear – I did not want
to rise and leave you so,
But the dead men's hands were beckoning
And I knew that I must go.

Ewart Alan Mackintosh, Seaforth Highlanders
Killed in Action 21 November 1917

On 4 August 1914, Great Britain declared war on Germany, and in the words of the foreign secretary Sir Edward Grey, the lights went out all over Europe. Hardly anyone had raised an eyebrow when an obscure Austrian Arch-Duke and his wife were assassinated by a Bosnian Serb with the unlikely name of Gavrilo Princip, in Sarajevo, a place few people had ever heard of. Austria however used the assassination to try and settle long-standing disputes with Serbia. Blaming Serbia for the Arch-Duke's murder, they presented her with a list of impossible demands, and when Serbia refused to acknowledge all these demands, Austria declared war. Now Germany had an alliance with Austria and felt obliged to support her. Russia, who had an alliance with Serbia, mobilised in her support. The French, seeing Germany mobilise on her very doorstep, also mobilised. Germany knew that in a European war France would be their biggest threat, and that a swift strike against the French would be necessary if they were to win a quick and decisive victory. To this end Germany launched the Schlieffen plan, which involved a gigantic westward sweep across Belgium and Luxembourg, followed by a wheel south into France; the whole operation was to take only forty-two days. Germany asked Belgium for free passage through their country and when this was refused, they invaded. Britain, who had a treaty with Belgium guaranteeing her neutrality, demanded Germany's immediate withdrawal and, when Germany refused, Britain declared war. Although many thought it would be a short war 'all over by Christmas' it was in fact to last for over four years, destroying a large slice of Europe and costing millions of lives.

In Britain it was a popular war and patriotism ran through the British and the empire like a fever as men flocked to enlist. The recruiting offices were full to bursting, Lord Kitchener's dream of a giant volunteer army 100,000-men strong was quickly realised and then surpassed. Until these raw recruits were fully trained, however, it would be up to the regular army and the partially trained territorials to hold the line.

The weather was glorious over that August bank holiday and the coastal resorts of Norfolk, such as Yarmouth, Cromer and Hunstanton, were full to overflowing. People were determined to enjoy themselves and laughter was the common denominator. Yarmouth had record crowds; mixed bathing had just been introduced and this new and exciting spectacle drew hundreds of straw-hatted voyeurs on to the promenade to watch the latest thing in sexual liberation. The only signs of the impending disaster were members of the Royal Garrison Artillery standing guard with bayonets fixed outside the old Coast Guard Station which was being used as the Royal Flying Corps Headquarters. Even this sight was turned into a tourist attraction as people crowded around to watch the changing of the guard. In the country men were out with their families, walking, cycling, playing games, picnicking or enjoying the annual work's outing; war was the last thing on most people's minds. Tom Williamson was in Yarmouth with his parents, enjoying a pint of ale and a freshly baked loaf in a local pub, Randall Cubitt spent the day with his family at Honing Hall, Captain Ward, the battalion's adjutant, had dinner with his brother-in-law Capt Mason at Necton Hall. At Sandringham, Frank Beck was at the centre of things as usual, helping to organise picnics and games for the estate workers. For thousands of families it was to be their last few moments of happiness as the inevitable telegrams began to arrive ordering them to report at once for duty.

The coastal resorts quickly emptied as men hurriedly returned home. There were strong rumours that the coastal towns were about to be invaded, bombarded by the German fleet (which did happen later in the war), or at the very least, turned into armed fortresses. Local trade slumped, forcing the mayor of Yarmouth to issue a statement telling people in the town to 'Keep Your Heads', following that up with a nationwide poster campaign reassuring would be holiday makers:

EVERYTHING AS USUAL.
RUMOURS ABSOLUTELY UNFOUNDED,
SPEND YOUR HOLIDAY AT GREAT YARMOUTH
OR GORLESTON AS ORIGINALLY INTENDED
David McCowan,
Mayor

One Yarmouth trader, sick of the accusations being made against him, placed the following ad in the local paper the *Yarmouth Mercury*:

TO THE EDITOR

Sir,

During the past week I have been caused considerable annoyance owing to a rumour being circulated in Gorleston that I displayed a notice on my premises advising visitors to quit the town within 48 hours.

The persons making such wild assertions are entirely misinformed, for no such ridiculous notice has ever been posted.

I do not wish to occupy too much of your valuable space, but feel sure you will give me an opportunity of denying such an untruth.

If those people who are busy with the tale will call upon me, I will go into details with them and explain the whole situation.

Thanking you.

Yours faithfully,
A.G. SIMMONS

Great excitement reigned in Yarmouth when a British destroyer brought in a German schooner. Local people rushed to the quayside to see the German crew as they were marched through the town and into captivity. There were also serious economic problems for the district as the fishing industry was brought to standstill and hundreds of men were made idle. Some went to help bring in the harvest while others enlisted, seeing it as a worthwhile alternative to unemployment or persuaded by a very effective campaign to encourage new recruitment.

TO THE LOYAL MEN OF NORFOLK

COME BACK TO THE COLOURS

All men under the age of 38 who have served in the regular army, military special reserve, volunteers or Territorial Forces are hereby invited to join the 5th Battalion Norfolk Regiment (Territorials)

YOUR COUNTRY NEEDS YOU

JOIN AT ONCE

GOD SAVE THE KING

Meanwhile as the civilian population were adjusting to the war the 5th Norfolks began to assemble. A military staff car arrived in the middle of the night at Church Farm Ridlington to take Lieutenant Randall Cubitt to his assembly point at Dereham. He dressed quickly and scribbled a short note to his father:

> Dear Squire,
>
> A motor came for me in [the] middle of night. I could not come to Honing.
>
> Say goodbye to all for present as I do not know when we go.
>
> At present, address Lieut Cubitt 5th Batt'n the Norfolks East-Dereham.
>
> Can you draw a cheque from fruit farm and give it to Cath, she has no money at present. You might have an eye to see that she is all right. If trouble? don't whatever you do kick up a fuss or encourage your men to; I mean if there is foreign fuss on coast.
>
> E.R.Cubitt
>
> My identity disc is in my draw, middle safe, can you send on to me.

Capt Frank Beck on receiving his telegram sent a quick explanatory note to Sir William Carington:

Sir

In my absence my wife is staying with Dr Moore at Virginia Water to help him.

She was very bright and helpful in this decision.

My brother will in my absence be virtually on the spot here and Kingston in the office.

My nephew Alec Beck who went through South Africa Campaign takes up a commission in this battalion in my company and I hope to leave here 10.00am sharp upon receipt of orders. I am sir,

Your obedient servant,

Frank Beck

12. *Private Tom Williamson as a seventeen-year-old territorial.*

Frank Beck then gathered his company together on the lawn of Laycocks, his house at Sandringham. He stood with Capt Knight, their backs to the house and overlooking the assembled men. Around the men stood their families, many of them crying, including Beck's five daughters. Beck then made a moving speech, telling the assembled crowd that he would look after the company and that they were to treat him as their father and he would bring them safely through the conflict. The men turned and, with Captain Beck at their head, marched away to the cheers and cries of the estate workers.

Meanwhile both Eustace and Victor Cubitt were hurrying home, Eustace from Ireland and Victor from Scotland, to meet up with their brother Randall. Alec Beck, dressed in a black bowler hat and suit, after making his goodbyes to his family, left Lord Mosley's estate in a small trap. He collected his friend, Second-Lieut Robert Adams, and made for the station. The locally based officers, like Major Woodwark, Capt Gay and Capt Mason, arrived at the drill hall in Dereham first and were briefed by Colonel Beauchamp and Adjutant Ward. Men began to pour in from every part of the county and even a few from outside it. The Yarmouth members of the battalion assembled at their drill hall and then marched to the town's railway station to the cheers of thousands of people who lined the way. As they proceeded they collected thirty new recruits, doubtless caught up in the euphoria of the moment.

As the various companies arrived at Dereham they were marched first to the Market Place and then to the Assembly Rooms where every man was examined by Doctors Belding, Howlett and Duigan, before being issued with rifles and one hundred rounds of ammunition. The only thing they had to provide for themselves were blankets, and the soldiers' families quickly supplied them. The Maltings, belonging to Messrs F.D.G. Smith Ltd, which was behind Dereham railway station, and the 'Old Mill' in Dereham, were requisitioned as sleeping quarters for the men, while the officers slept on the top floor of the warehouse of Hobbies Ltd. During the day the men assembled at the Corn Hall, the Masonic Hall and the Assembly Rooms, for their daily briefings and orders.

After two weeks at Dereham the battalion was transferred to Billericay, and from there they marched to Colchester, a distance of over twenty miles. This march was undertaken on one of the hottest days of August and a number of the battalion collapsed *en route*. During the march the battalion was accosted by a drunk by the name of Walter Henson who waved his arms around and shouted, 'You are only blooming territorials, blooming rotters, you are cowards, if you saw a German you would run away, blooming slaves'. The men soon got sick of this and after a short chase the man was arrested by Major Woodwark and two of his company. He was later fined ten shillings for being drunk and disorderly and apologised to Colonel Beauchamp.

In August 1914, they were visited by Sir Ian Hamilton, a man who was to play an important part later in their story. After inspecting them he wrote to King George V's private secretary Lord Stamfordham at Buckingham Palace:

> My dear Stamfordham,
>
> Even in these dreadfully anxious and momentous times I think it is possible that the King might like to hear what a fine appearance the Sandringham Company of the 5th Norfolks put in when I yesterday inspected them near Colchester. They stood 100 on parade and the officer commanding the company said he expected to be 120 strong in three days' time. Every single individual of all ranks has volunteered for service overseas, and a finer, smarter, keener looking lot of young soldiers it would be difficult to find.
>
> Believe me,
>
> Yours sincerely,
>
> IAN HAMILTON

On arrival at Colchester the men were billeted in a church in the grounds of an asylum, while the officers were given rooms in the hospital itself, some of the inmates being moved out to provide room. In the church the men slept two to a pew and the officers and NCOs would announce their orders regarding rations, sentry duties and the day's training from the pulpit. Parades caused all sorts of embarrassment as the hospital's inmates, who had no respect for anybody, watched on and heckled the battalion. On one occasion when Colonel Beauchamp was taking the parade a voice from among the hospital inmates screamed, 'Oh, you dirty old man, you revolting old thing – you say it's by the right and you know it's all wrong'. This was followed by screams of abuse of every kind. There was one company commander who was always immaculately turned out and not a little pleased with himself. He really suffered. As soon as he appeared on the parade ground, the inmates would start screaming at him, 'peacock about nothing' and other abusive remarks. The battalion remained in the church until Christmas 1914, when they were moved to empty four-roomed bungalows at Boxted, two men to a room with a cook house situated outside. Food was scarce and their main meal consisted of one loaf between eight, with a small allowance of meat or fish. At Christmas the men decorated their rooms and some got special home leave. One corporal, returning from leave the worse for drink, tried to set fire to some of the decorations in Tom Williamsons' house. When Tom tried to stop him, he pointed a revolver at Tom's head and threatened to shoot him. Finally however Tom managed to calm him down and the man fell onto his bed in a drunken stupor.

It was while at Colchester that Second-Lieut Rolland Pelly was commissioned into the battalion; he recounts the event vividly in his diary:

13. King George V meeting Captain Frank Beck and the Sandringham Company at Colchester in November 1914 (Beck Collection).

> At Christmas I volunteered. My brother-in-law, Randall Cubitt, was a Territorial in the 5th Norfolks and was stationed at Colchester. I bicycled over there from Cambridge to see the Commanding Officer Sir Horace Beauchamp. He was so impressed at anyone bicycling fifty miles and fifty miles back to see him that he nominated me for a commission on the spot. I was gazetted Second-Lieut in January 1915.

The battalion's days consisted of route marches, shooting, bayonet practice, and field exercises practising attacking and defending a variety of positions. On one occasion Second-Lieut Rolland Pelly's platoon commander was away and Pelly was obliged to lead a route march riding his commander's horse. He made a note of the incident in his diary:

> It was bad enough to be in charge of the Company, but worse to be riding, of which I had little experience. Suddenly the company behind me started singing 'A little Child Shall Lead Them.' I felt so embarrassed! I turned in my saddle and shouted back 'Yes, but he'll jolly well ride on a horse,' which pleased them mightily. Oh, the agony of those route marches – twenty miles at a time – especially on the men's feet. The officer's job seemed largely to consist of carrying the heavy equipment of men who fell out as well as their own.

Training and the constant route marches were not without their tragedies. Late during the summer, after a particularly difficult march on a swelteringly hot day, two men of the Norfolks, while returning to their billets, found a barrel of what they thought was cider outside a cottage door. They were both thirsty and drank deeply. In spite of having a doctor close by and receiving prompt medical attention both died: unfortunately it had not been cider but weed killer that they had drunk.

While at Colchester the battalion was visited by King George V, who was two hours late; the Norfolks had to stand on parade in the pouring rain awaiting his arrival. He finally inspected the battalion and expressed great delight at seeing the Sandringham company and his old friend and agent, Frank Beck once again.

The battalion was still not at full strength and recruiting and training was still going on apace. It was Major Woodwark and his never-ending stream of ideas that played an important part in both these activities. After arriving in Colchester he went from company to company selecting soldiers who could play a variety of musical instruments and formed a battalion band. In company with Capt Coxon and the band's conductor, Band Master Dines, he travelled the length and breadth of the county with them giving concerts and making rousing patriotic speeches in market places, schools and Town Halls, desperately trying to enlist new recruits. Their success varied considerably; at Fincham and Stoke Ferry, despite a good turn out, they did not manage to recruit a single man, however at both Downham and Swaffham they were luckier and managed to persuade twenty new men to join up. Inter-battalion and company sports like football and athletics became very popular and important to unit prestige. With so many former professional and amateur footballers in the 5th Norfolks they had a record second to none and lost very few matches. Their most important match was probably against Lynn Athletic, which was played at Felixstow before a crowd of some 3,000 spectators. Major Woodwark kicked off and the 5th Norfolks finally won a hard fought competition by four goals to two. There were also several inter-company athletic competitions which 'F' company tended to win. Major Woodwark displayed a remarkable turn of speed during both the hundred-yard sprint and the mile, being unbeaten throughout the Norfolks' training.

From Colchester the Battalion were moved to Bury-St-Edmunds by train. *En route* private Tom Williamson lost his hat while leaning out of a carriage window. The following day he went on parade with a reserve's blue cap. When Colonel Beauchamp saw him he was given sentry duty every week on successive nights. By now Second-Lieut Pelly had managed to get hold of a motor cycle and endeavoured to get away as often as possible to visit family and friends in the local area. Capt Pattrick managed to get time off to give away his sister in marriage to Lieut Malcolm Clark. There was also a small rebellion amongst the officers against the battalion's Commanding Officer Colonel Beauchamp, in whom a number of the officers had lost confidence. Colonel Beauchamp, as a former cavalry officer, was finding it increasingly difficult to manage an infantry battalion. The leader of this rebellion was the Adjutant Capt 'Ginger' Ward who was still furious at what he considered to be the insult of being attached to a mere territorial battalion and he was always in a foul temper with everybody. It was finally decided that Colonel Beauchamp should continue to command the battalion as long as all his orders were written by Capt Ward.

While posted at Bury-St-Edmunds the battalion was attacked by a German bomber and came very close to having all its officers killed when the hotel in which they were billeted suffered a direct hit. Fortunately the officers were out at the time of the attack and no casualties were sustained. The men were billeted with local families and treated very well indeed, having their first comfortable quarters since the war began.

From Bury-St-Edmunds the Norfolks were transferred to Watford where they became part of 54th (East Anglian) Division and together with the 5th Suffolks and 8th Hampshires formed the 163rd Infantry Brigade. While the battalion was awaiting further orders the Great Eastern Railway gave a tea party at the James Restaurant for all their former employees and their families serving with the 5th Norfolks and promised them all secure jobs on their return from the front. Capt Beck returned to Sandringham for a short while to make sure that everything was running smoothly While there, and realising that it could not be long before they would be sent overseas, he felt obliged to ask the King's permission to return to the battalion. He wrote to the Rt Hon. Sir Fredrick Ponsonby:

> Sir,
>
> I would be grateful if you would ask the King's consent for me to return to the Regiment in a week or a fortnight's time according to the likely time we leave for abroad ... If the company has the opportunity of serving their King in the field the after effect will have a very good influence on the estate for many years.
>
> You know I hate leaving my work here again but my brother will be only too pleased, I know, to try and earn more fully the more than generous present His Majesty has already given him. For myself I will try very hard to bring credit on the Sandringham Estate together with my men.
>
> I would be very glad if you could first ascertain privately from the War Office if Sir Horace Beauchamp is informed correctly as to the probability of an early move for our Battalion ...
>
> I am sir
>
> Your obedient servant
>
> Frank Beck.

Sir Fredrick Ponsonby replied two days later:

> I submitted to the King your letter, together with the enclosure from Sir Horace Beauchamp. His Majesty said that he quite understands your desire to go with the Sandringham company, and he thought you should therefore return in good time, so as to be in touch with the Company before they leave. Will you tell Sir Horace Beauchamp that The King wishes you to stop at Sandringham for another ten days, but after that you will return to your battalion, unless of course the orders are altered in any way. If there is any chance of the departure of the battalion taking place at an earlier date you should take steps to ensure that you are not left behind.
>
> Yours truly,
>
> F.E.G. Ponsonby

Frank Beck replied to Sir Fredrick Ponsonby at once:

> Sir
>
> Thank you very much for your letter. I am arranging to rejoin my company in ten days time. Will you please convey to the King my most dutiful thanks …
>
> I trust that France may be our goal though it matters not where we go so long as we mettle which I trust we may do.
>
> I am
>
> Your faithful servant
>
> Frank Beck

Shortly before embarking, the Sandringham Company received a telegram from King George V:

> My best wishes to you and to the Sandringham Company on the eve of your departure for the front. I have known you all for many years and am confident that the same spirit of loyalty and patriotism, in which you answered the call to arms, will inspire your deeds in the face of the enemy. May God bless and protect you
>
> George RI

14. Sandringham Company in tropical uniform 1915'

The Sandringham company replied:

> The Sandringham Company send most loyal and heartfelt thanks for Your Majesty's most kind message. Their one desire is to prove themselves worthy of their King.

By now the battalion knew its destination, it was not France and the Western Front but a small peninsula in Northern Turkey called Gallipoli. It was a place that few of the battalion had ever heard of, but for those that survived it was to be a place that none of them would ever forget.

Chapter five

Gallipoli: The Campaign

> The drama of the Dardanelles campaign by reason of the beauty of its setting, the grandeur of its theme and the unhappiness of its ending, will always rank amongst the world's classic tragedies. The story is a record of lost opportunities and eventual failure; yet it is a story which men of British race may ponder if not without pain, yet certainly not without pride; for amidst circumstances of unsurpassed difficulty and strain, the bravery, fortitude and stoical endurance of the invading troops upheld most worthily the high traditions of the fighting services of the Crown.
>
> Official History

In March 1911 Winston Churchill wrote a cabinet memorandum regarding the forcing of the Dardanelles from the sea, 'it should be remembered,' he wrote, 'that it is no longer possible to force the Dardanelles, and nobody should expose a modern fleet to such peril.' How quickly he was to change his mind.

Although the Gallipoli peninsula belongs to Europe it is separated from Asia by only a narrow strip of water some forty miles long which links the Aegean Sea and the sea of Marmara. At its western mouth the Dardanelles is only some 4000 yards wide and is guarded by the fortresses of Sedd el Bahr and Kum Kale. The channel then widens for about four miles, but by the time it reaches the narrows it is only 1,600 yards across with the Kilid Bahr plateau to the west and the town of Cannakkale (Chanak on the British maps of 1915) to the east. The peninsula itself is approximately fifty-five miles long and it is only 140 miles from Cape Helles and its southernmost tip to Istanbul (Constantinople). In the spring and early summer the peninsula is beautiful, the hills are ablaze with wild flowers and birds dart in and out of the gullies and ravines that seem to litter the area. As the summer draws on, however, the grass dies, everything begins to look withered and parched, and a film of dust settles over the entire landscape. In the winter the climate contrasts again and it becomes extremely cold

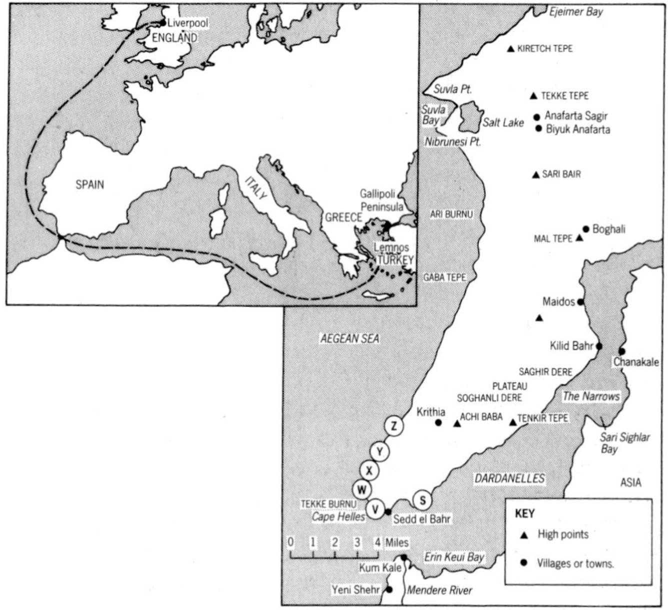

15. Map of the Gallipoli Peninsula.

with severe snow storms and heavy rains which turn gentle streams into raging torrents. The Suvla plain with its giant salt lake, which is to play an important part in our story, lies to the north of the Sari Bair hills. The plain is overlooked by the Kiretch Tepe and Tekke Tepe heights which form a semi-circle around the bay. Looking down upon this scene, it has the appearance of a huge natural arena and it was to be the stage for one of the First War's greatest tragedies.

During the nineteenth century Britain helped to preserve the Ottoman Empire as a barrier against Russian ambitions in the Mediterranean. However, largely due to British public revulsion against Turkish atrocities, firstly in Bulgaria and later in Armenia, relations began to cool. As a result Turkey began to foster closer relations with Germany, who provided a military mission between 1883 and 1895; hundreds of Turkish officers were trained in Germany, trade between the two countries increased, and the Kaiser made a state visit to Constantinople. Russia was content to leave her ambitions towards Turkey alone as long as she maintained her link with the Mediterranean through the straits. In 1908 Sultan Abdul Hamid was deposed by a group of young army officers calling themselves the 'Young Turks' who were determined to liberalise Turkish society. However as the Ottoman empire collapsed so did the Young Turks' idealistic liberal experiment. Germany was quick to adapt to the new Turkish situation and secured a military mission headed by General Liman Von Sanders.

Even with such strong German influence it was by no means certain that Turkey would enter the war on the side of Germany in August 1914. What finally decided it was a series of diplomatic blunders by the British. First they refused to hand over two Turkish battleships the *Sultan Osman* and the *Reshadieh*, that were being built in British shipyards. This decision caused a wave of anti-British feeling throughout Turkey. Again the Germans were quick to react and, after being chased through the Mediterranean by part of the British fleet, the battleships *Goeben* and *Breslau* steamed into the straits and were presented to the Turkish government as replacements. Then in September 1914 a British naval squadron close to the entrance of the straits ordered a Turkish torpedo boat to turn back. This gave the Germans the opportunity they were looking for and they pursuaded the Turkish Admiralty to close the straits and lay mines. Russia's vital life-line had been broken and her ships had to return to port. German influence over Turkey now became stronger and on 28 October the Turkish government finally took sides and the Turkish fleet bombarded the Russian ports of Odessa and Sebastopol, and Turkey declared war on 31 October 1914.

Within the first three months of the war allied casualties reached almost a million. Stagnation had set in on the Western Front, trench systems stretched for 350 miles from the North sea to the Swiss Alps. On 25 November 1914, during a meeting of the War Council, Winston Churchill brought forward the idea of a joint military and naval attack on the Dardanelles to try and put Turkey out of the war, open up a supply route to Russia and possibly open another front against the Germans. It was finally decided, despite reservations from a number of people, to launch a combined French and British naval assault against the Dardanelles in an effort to force a passage through them before bombarding Constantinople and forcing the Turkish government to surrender. At 9.51 am on 19 February 1915 the assault began. However the weather was bad, the Turks elusive and the failure of the Navy to silence the Turkish guns further up the straits meant that the minesweepers could not do their job and, until they could, the task force could not sail into the straits. The next attack came on 18 March. All went well at first with only minor damage to the ships and a considerable amount of damage done to the Turkish defences. Then the French ship *Bouvet* hit a mine, turned over and sank with over 600 hands. The minesweepers were again moved forward but failed to clear all the mines. The *Inflexible* then began to list to starboard – also having hit a mine. Somehow she managed to limp to a safe port. The *Irresistible* was the next to be mined, followed by the *Ocean*. Both ships later sank and the naval operation was called off.

The second phase was a combined naval and land operation but this took time to organise and security was poor. The German General Liman Von Sanders had time to repair and improve his defences and Mustafa Kemal Pasha (later the president of Turkey and probably the most famous of all Turkish generals), was able to take charge of the Turkish forces in the peninsula. Although morale was high amongst the Turkish soldiers following their victory, it was equally high amongst the British. There was an air of excitement about the 'Constantinople Expedition' amongst the young, classically educated Oxbridge officers; the idea of fighting a war on the plains of Troy was 'too wonderful for belief'. The young Cambridge poet Rupert Brooke probably summed up their feelings when he wrote,

> I had not imagined fate could be so kind … Will hero's tower crumble under the 15-inch guns? Will the sea be polyphloisbic

> and wine-dark and unvintageable? Shall I loot mosaics from St. Sophia, and Turkish Delight and carpets? Should we be the turning point in history? Oh god! I've never been quite so happy in my life I think. Never quite so pervasively happy; like a stream flowing entirely to one end. I suddenly realized that the ambition of my life has been – since I was two – to go on a military expedition against Constantinople.

General Sir Ian Hamilton who had been selected to be the Commander-in-Chief of the land expedition, was also excited about the campaign and in his ability to change the course of the war. He wrote in his diary,

> Once in a generation a mysterious wish for war passes through the people. Their instinct tells them that there is no other way of progress and escape from habits that no longer fit them. Whole generations of statesmen will fumble over reforms for a lifetime which are put into full-blooded execution within a week of a declaration of war. There is no other way. Only by intense suffering can the nation grow, just as a snake once a year must with anguish slough off the once beautiful coat which has now become a straitjacket.

The thousands of men who formed the rank and file while less poetical were no less ardent, and although for most of them it would be their first taste of battle they were determined to be brave.

The attacking force was a mixed bag indeed. There were French Zouaves and Foreign Legionaries from Africa, Sikhs and Gurkhas from India, Levantine Jews and Greeks; sailors from both the British and French Navies as well as English, Scottish and Irish troops; finally there were the New Zealanders and Australians, the famous ANZACS. General Hamilton had some 75,000 men at his disposal: 30,000 Australians divided into two divisions, 17,000 men of the 29th Division, one French division of 16,000 men and a Royal Naval Division of 10,000 men. These men were supported by 1,600 horses, donkeys and mules and over 300 vehicles. Hamilton's plan amounted to a simple assault upon the Gallipoli peninsula itself. The main attacking force would go ashore at five small beaches at Cape Helles at the extreme tip of the peninsula. The Anzacs would land between Gaba Tepe and Fisherman's Hut and try to get behind the Turkish defenders at Cape Helles. Meanwhile the Royal Naval Division and the French would make a diversionary attack at Bulair and Kum Kale; later both these forces would be returned to the main attack.

The attack went ahead on 25 April 1915. The British landed on beaches numbered by the initials S,V,W,X,Y, and Z. Altogether eighty-four British regiments landed. At Anzac cove, due to strong currents, thousands of Australian and New Zealand troops were landed in the wrong place and despite outstanding bravery suffered hundreds of casualties. Although the British managed to land almost without opposition on a number of the beaches like 'Y' and 'X', it was a different story elsewhere. The Lancashire Fusiliers landed at 'W' beach and were slaughtered, suffering 500 casualties out of their landing force of 950 and earning 6 VCs before breakfast. As the old steamship the *River Clyde*, the Trojan horse of the expedition, approached 'V' beach the men concealed inside her hull and in the boats being towed behind waited patiently to land. It was a fine Mediterranean morning, the sea was calm and as still as a millpond. As the *River Clyde*'s bows grounded, the Turkish soldiers who had remained concealed until the last moment opened fire with machine guns and rifle fire. The men cramped into the boats behind the *River Clyde* were killed where they sat and the boats drifted away. The men inside the *River Clyde* were shot as they ran down the gangway in a desperate effort to get ashore. The element of surprise had gone and both sides began to mass men on to the field of battle, the Turks determined to throw the British back into the sea and the British determined to secure the straits and fight their way to Constantinople. As long as these hopes remained the slaughter would continue. The campaign now became bogged down until it was not unlike the situation on the Western Front. If the allies were to gain the early victory they had hoped for they would have to break out into the peninsula.

A fresh landing on the Turkish coast was decided upon and once again the landing had to be in the peninsula. A plan was eventually conceived: the Anzacs were to assault Chunuk Bair, having first made a feint at a place called Lone Pine, simultaneously there was to be a new landing at Suvla Bay. It was hoped that these combined attacks would capture the hills surrounding the area and then push through to the Narrows about four miles further on. With the Turkish army now bottled up in the peninsula it was hoped that this would bring a quick end to the campaign. Suvla Bay was the perfect place for the landings. It offered a safe anchorage, the area was known to be lightly defended and the salt lake which was about a mile-and-a-half wide was known to dry up during the summer. Everything depended upon the speed of the attack and the advance inland to join up with Birdwood fighting the main battle on Sari Bair. The day of the attack was fixed for 6 August. Three ocean-going liners, the *Olympic, Mauretania* and the *Aquitania* were chartered to bring the 25,000 fresh troops from Britain – mainly territorials and Kitchener's men – that would be required for the plan to succeed.

At first the landings at Suvla were an unqualified success with few casualties, but instead of immediately moving forward to take advantage of this early success they spent twenty-four hours in re-organising the landing beaches, and at the end of the first day the British at Suvla had barely advanced two miles inland. This delay gave the Turks time to reorganise themselves and thousands of Turkish troops poured into the area. The British started to suffer serious casualties and it was into this confusion that the 5th Norfolks were landed together with thousands of other territorials in an attempt to try and capture objectives which could have been taken quite easily within hours of the initial landings.

Chapter six

Foreign Fields

Fair broke the day this morning,
Against the Dardanelles;
The breeze blew soft, the morn's cheeks
were cold as cold as sea-shells.

But other shells are waiting
Across the Aegean Sea,
Shrapnel and high explosive
Shells and hells for me.

Lieut-Cmdr Patrick Shaw-Stewart
Royal Naval Div – K.I.A. 1917

At 12 noon on 29 July 1915, the 5th battalion of the Norfolk regiment embarked on the SS *Aquitania* at Liverpool in company with thousands of other troops including the 4th Norfolks. The SS *Aquitania* was one of the largest luxury ocean-going liners afloat. She had been built in 1914 at Clydebank for the Cunard line, she was almost 45,000 tons and 866 feet in length. Her role in life was to take distinguished fare-paying passengers, first class, to exotic destinations of their choice. This time the passengers, although no less distinguished, were being taken to a destination certainly not exotic and definitely not of their choice.

The first problem to beset the battalion was that not a single 'Brass Hat' had gone forward to superintend the embarkation and as a result it was a disorganised shambles. The ship's embarkation officer was a much-harried old man more used to the loading of holiday makers' suitcases than military stores. His idea of loading a ship was to get the battalion's stores on board as quickly as possible and in any order, with the minimum of fuss or for that matter care. As a result, the entrenching tools and signalling apparatus, some of the battalions most important and delicate equipment, which just happened to come off the train first, were pitched into the bottom of the ships hold and the heavy equipment, such as field cookers, machinegun wagons and limbers were placed on top, making it almost impossible to retrieve them. The ship's purser, on seeing the field cookers being loaded, grinned sardonically and remarked, 'They won't go further than Lemnos with you, from there they will be shipped to Alexandria and turned out onto the beach to rust.' Such was the fate of hundreds of tons of military equipment. Attempts were made to recover the entrenching tools from the bottom of the ship's hold but the Captain said it was impossible and they would have to remain there until the end of the voyage. However, Major Woodwark, known throughout the battalion as a businessman, and a very persuasive person, became friendly with one of the ship's officers and with a bit of 'talking to' prevailed upon him to open the hatchway and managed to recover both the entrenching tools and the signalling apparatus.

At 11pm on 30 July 1915 the SS *Aquitania* slipped her mooring and with thousands of soldiers lining her decks waving, singing and cheering to the people on the quayside she steamed out of Liverpool under a full moon and slipped into the Irish Sea heading for the Dardanelles. For many hundreds of men it was to be their last glimpse of England.

Private Walter Rowe, 5th Norfolks, kept a diary of the voyage:

> July 29th. We left … at 4am and after a train ride of seven hours we found ourselves on the docks at Liverpool. We then had to march for almost fifteen minutes to the transport ship Aquitania. She is a huge ship and her interior is fitted up like a palace. We are very fortunate in having her for our transport, as we are able to have every convenience. When one is in the dining saloon one imagines one self to be in a large hotel. The ship is also very speedy and travels remarkably smoothly and easily.
>
> July 30th. In the morning the ship was still in the dock, but in the afternoon she moved into the river. We left about eleven o'clock and the trip down the river in the moonlight was a very enjoyable.
>
> July 31st. We are now getting out into the Atlantic and beginning to feel the rollers. We have not seen any submarines yet. The rough weather made a good many of the men sea-sick. Later in the evening we got near the Bay of Biscay, only of course, we are well out in the ocean. We have practice every day in taking our place near the lifeboats,

allotted to us in case of emergency.

August 1st. The rough weather continues. We had church parade during the morning.

August 2nd. We are now having glorious weather. During the morning we passed near the spot where the battle of Trafalgar was fought. In the afternoon we sighted the coast of Spain the first land we have seen since leaving England. About 4.30pm we passed Gibraltar. The land on each side of the strait is very mountainous and here and there we saw small towns in which all the buildings seemed to be built of white stone.

August 3rd. The weather is glorious. Here in the Mediterranean the sea is practically smooth and a glorious blue in colour. We have passed several ships but none of them can touch us with regards to speed. We lost sight of land again about noon. Every now and again we pass shoals of porpoises which we can see quite plainly playing in the water.

August 5th. We are finding the weather very hot, and are going about very scantily clad. Yesterday we passed several islands including Malta. All we saw of the latter was steep cliffs with a few houses scattered on top. We have seen one or two warships but they are generally a long way off. We are nearing our destination now. We expect to reach Lemnos to-morrow morning. From there it is about an hours run to the Gallipoli Peninsula. We leave the ship at Lemnos.

During the voyage the troops' main problem was getting sufficient water to drink and many of the troops seemed to suffer from a continuous thirst. The organisation on board the ship was not all that it could be and as if to emphasise the inefficient way the ship was run, ridiculous orders were often given. The one that seems to have been remembered best was the order regarding the water taps. It was decided that every water tap on the *Aquitania* was to be inspected every hour and then a report made to the Captain on the bridge. It was an impossible order to carry out and was, like many similar orders simply ignored. As the SS *Aquitania* made her way slowly but surely towards its destination it encountered several storms and the sea became very rough. The battalion's machine-guns, which were stacked on the deck, broke loose and crashed, first to one side of the ship and then the other. It was only by inspired efforts and great good fortune that Second-Lieut Pelly, who was the battalion's Orderly Officer, only lost two guns overboard. The storms also caused a great deal of sickness amongst the troops and hundreds of men became ill both from the effects of the rough sea and typically as a result of reaction to the sea-sickness pills issued before the trip. It wasn't only the weather that was causing problems. The *Aquitania*'s escort of destroyers were having trouble keeping up, and began to loose touch with her, and so the ship had to depend on her speed to evade attention from German submarines, which roamed the Mediterranean looking for easy and important targets. Despite the ship's speed however, the SS *Aquitania* was attacked but fortunately the torpedoes missed and the submarine was finally chased off by the escorting destroyers. During this attack one of the ships steward's collapsed and had to be taken to his quarters. It was later learnt that he had been on board the Cunard liner *Lusitania* when she had been torpedoed by the U-20 on 7 May 1915 with the loss of 1,198 men, women and children.

Keeping thousands of men occupied in such a confined space was another difficulty. The men were supposed to swim every day but due to the number of soldiers on board, these swims had to be taken in company order and the 5th Norfolks only managed two forty-five minute sessions throughout their long voyage. There was regular PT and the Regimental Sergt-Major drilled the battalion every day, and there was a fully equipped gym, again only occasionally available due to the large demand for its facilities. The one thing that everybody seemed to enjoy was the military band that played during the afternoon and evening; the most popular request being *Are we all here?*. The ship continued to zigzag its way towards Gallipoli. On 1 August it passed through the Bay of Biscay, on the 2nd they sighted Gibralter, on the 3rd there was an air of excitement as the men collect their £1 pay, the last they would receive until they returned home again. On 4 August they passed Malta and had an interdenominational church service to commemorate the anniversary of the outbreak of war. 'In spite,' as Second-Lieut Pelly observed 'of seeing Africa before Spain', the ship reached Imbros in five days arriving on 6 August 1915.

Two days later on Sunday 8 August 1915, Lieut Victor Cubitt wrote home:

> Dear Mum,
>
> We are still in the harbour but expect to go forward sometime this week but it may be a very long time before we see any fighting. The news we get here is exceedingly good and

everyone is in the best of spirits. We are all flourishing

Nothing more for now

Your loving son,

VICTOR

On 9 August, the battalion, together with the 4th Norfolks and the 8th Hampshires, transferred to the SS *Osmaih*, leaving three officers and 157 men behind to follow later. Instead of being moved forward straight away the battalion were ordered to remain on board the ship overnight. The *Osmaih* was carrying 1700 troops but had accommodation for only 800 and the men had to lie down where and when they could. Few were able to wash and latrines were woefully insufficient. Sergt Smith of D company became the battalion's favourite when he managed to commandeer nine out of the twenty cans of coffee and about half the bread, providing a sumptuous breakfast for both officers and men. The 4th Norfolks, whose officers had overslept, were very upset to find that all the coffee had gone, but the 5th took pity on them and gave them their remaining tins. Capt Gay, the battalion's Mess President, showed his worth when he managed to retrieve three boxes of the battalion's stores from the ship's hold before they steamed off towards Lemnos.

The 5th battalion soon came in sight of the island of Imbros close to the Turkish mainland and could hear and see the shells bursting on Achi Baba. It was their first sight and sound of war and most of them found it very difficult to believe that it was all happening within a few miles of their position.

Major Purdy described the scene:

> The sun was going down behind Samothrace which rose sheer out of the sea behind Imbros a vast cone shaped mass of purple all soft and shadowy in the evening light, while the level rays of the sun fell eastwards clear and bright on the round hill of Tenedos and the red coast of Asia behind. To the North the guns thundered, but the puffs of smoke on the hills looked fat and lazy as they slowly floated up into the sky, it seemed impossible that they should be to those beneath them the black pall of shattering death.

***16.** Major Purdy.*

They passed through the minefield and anchored in Imbros Harbour. Imbros was crowded with liners, tramps, monitors, submarines, cruisers and battleships of every type and description. One large liner close to the shore had sunk by her stern and her rails were just visible above the water. As night drew on, the hospital ships with their green lights from bow to stern and the bright Red Cross amidships made the whole picture seem like a scene from a fairytale, or as Major Purdy wrote in his diary, 'to compare great things with small, a scene on a modern stage'.

Second-Lieut Rolland Pelly wrote to his father describing the scene:

> It is a lovely day, at present we do nothing but walk round the ship or look at battleships all round. You couldn't find a calmer more peaceful spot. It is a fairly large island and looks pretty bleak à la Scotland. There are little native sailing boats about and I hope if we stay that I shall get to sail. One came along

side just now with two natives and its name was APKA..IA. So they still stick to those old letters!

Well best love

Rolland

In the evening the stores that Capt Gay had managed to recover were opened and the company officers enjoyed a meal of sardines, tongue, cake, marmalade and Greek bread, all washed down with whisky and soda at 1s 3d a glass.

On 10 August the battalion steamed out of harbour in the direction of Suvla Bay. Private Cliff Harrison remembers the men of the battalion were in the best of moods, singing, joking and laughing. As they approached land they could see other transports close to shore. There were three or four cruisers and monitors at the south end of the bay firing inland, their shells bursting on top of a high ridge which they later discovered to be Hill 971. They could now also hear the rattle of machine-gun fire. On a bluff close to the shore and just north of the Southern Horn of the Bay were numbers of troops and mules, some halted, some moving forward. A British battery was firing continuously towards the Turkish positions as it had been since it landed three days previously. To the left of the Bay, near its north-western point, troops were landing from lighters and pushing inland.

The battalion's ship anchored at about 4pm half a mile from the shore and there they stayed watching the continuing battle inland as Anafarta was pounded by fourteen-inch shells and large columns of smoke and debris rose up from time to time among its houses. In due course a lighter came alongside and both A and D and some of C company climbed on board and were taken to the landing stages at 'A' Beach. The battalion finally landed on Turkish soil at 5.30am on 10 August 1915. On landing, Private John Dye of the Sandringham Company remembers remarking to his Commanding Officer, Capt Frank Beck, 'I don't think we are going to be made very welcome here sir.' Beck laughed and replied 'I don't thing we will, Dye.' Despite the fact that many of the men were still suffering the effects of a long and uncomfortable sea journey and the after effects of the inoculations they received before leaving England, they were ordered to move forward. Each man was issued with two pints of water which they were told had to last for three days and it was suggested that they keep a small pebble in their mouth. Great care had to be taken not to stand on land mines, which were still causing casualties amongst British troops. Later that day, the battalion piled arms, removed their equipment and bivouacked, settling down to get what rest they could as the temperature began to rise. Major Purdy later wrote in his diary that the vegetation reminded him of that at Blakeney Point, an area he loved and a popular Norfolk beauty spot.

Later still Capt Bridgwater, the battalion's Staff Captain, asked for two senior officers to go with him on a reconnaissance. Major Purdy and Capt Knight volunteered and set off together with Captains Oliver and Fisher from the Suffolks (three of the officers all being Old Haileyburians). After passing the blackened bodies of several Turkish soldiers and inspecting captured Turkish trenches, they found a company of Lancashires lying along the bed of a dry watercourse which they had roughly entrenched. The subaltern in command told the party that the firing line was about half a mile in front of their position and that they had been heavily sniped at all day. The valley to their right was full of snipers who were wonderfully camouflaged and difficult to spot. Some of the Turkish soldiers had even dressed themselves as pigs in order to get close to the British lines, and would let the British troops pass their position before opening fire. He also observed, to the officers' amazement, that it was believed that some of the Turkish army's best snipers were women.

Major Purdy and Capt Knight returned to the battalion and at 9pm the battalion received orders to stand to. The Suffolks moved off and the Norfolks followed, together with the 8th battalion of the Hampshire Regiment. Conditions were so bad that the battalion was forced to stop every ten minutes to rest. They also became separated and several companies became totally lost. At 1am D company finally found their position, followed by C company a short time later. B and A companies finally found the rest of the battalion some considerable time later. The battalion lay down in two ranks with bayonets fixed and a couple of listening posts about fifty yards in front of each company. As Major Purdey lay there with his men he observed the strange smells that the wind blew across his position, delicious spicy smells from some of the local plants combined with the loathsome sickly smell of hundreds of unburied bodies. A Lance-Corp of A company wrote home to his parents describing the conditions.

> At 5am the battalion breakfasted on bully beef and biscuits and did what they could to keep warm in the intense cold of the Turkish nights. After breakfast orders were received to advance in line of platoons in double file. The going was rough over rocky ground with dried up watercourses running from the high ground on their left to the Salt Lake. Everything was covered with thick scrub. This scrub consisted of bushes with leaves like a holly and just as prickly, but also with acorns in prickly cups and growing four or five feet high and very thick making it difficult and painful to push through. After a while the terrain changed and became cultivated with small fields of three to four acres which had been roughly ploughed. These fields were surrounded by low fences and deep ditches. Along these fences were small bushy oaks with big trunks and wide spreading branches, dark leaves and acorn set in a huge cup of fleshy tentacles [believed to be Valonea Oaks].
>
> As the brigade advanced it was also subjected to shell fire from their own ships. As shells exploded above their heads and showered them with shrapnel they were forced to take cover in a deep ditch where they lay for over an hour. As a result of this shelling the battalion suffered six casualties, fortunately none serious. One shell exploded just above the heads of Captains Knight and Birkbeck knocking them down, but despite Birkbeck's glasses being smashed, by some miracle neither of the men was injured.

The battalion dug themselves in as best they could and settled down. Lance-Corporal Seaman later wrote home to his parents:

> Just a few lines to let you know that I am all right. Our boys are keeping a good spirit. The weather is causing a lot of trouble. In the day time we can't for the life of us keep cool, and at night we want about four blankets to keep the cold out. The other day the Turks pounded a lot of shrapnel into us in return for some explosives we had presented them with. This was falling in the midst of us, and one shrapnel bullet had the sauce to hit the biscuit tin I was sitting on at the time.

Collecting sufficient water for the battalion was a constant problem, the nearest source being a water hole, about eight feet deep with brown and murky water. The doctor gave the all-clear to drink it, but it was mainly used for washing and shaving. The only alternative was a clear water well back at the beach where they had originally landed, but this was over a mile and a half away and both difficult and dangerous to get to. Despite this, runners were sent out to fill as many water bottles as possible. Later quarter-master Sergt Smith and the fatigue party which had been left behind on the *Osmaih* joined the battalion, bringing with them the battalion's rum rations, although, as one officer observed 'we would have preferred water'. The smell from a dead horse which lay in a field only a few yards from the battalion's position caused great offence until Capt Frank Beck and some of the men from the Sandringham Company removed it. It was a beautiful animal which had been killed by shell fire from the British guns, and the death of such a fine animal caused a great deal of upset amongst the farming fraternity of the Norfolk men. The Norfolks were constantly sniped at, but despite the bullets singing over their heads and 'phitting' into the ground around the battalion and the constant noise of battle, the area was full of wildlife. The men observed hares, hawks and snakes, and Sergt John Goulder, a game keeper on a Norfolk estate, swore that he heard some partridges. The sun was unbearably hot and the men had to find what shelter they could to protect themselves from its burning rays. Flies and insects of all types swarmed around the men's position making it almost impossible to eat or drink. One veteran remembered the conditions:

> Immediately I opened my tin of jam the flies rushed it … all fighting amongst themselves. I wrapped my overcoat over the tin and gouged out the flies, then spread the jam on my biscuit holding my hand over it, and drew the biscuit out of the coat. As I began to eat my biscuit a lot of flies flew into my mouth and beat about inside. I nearly howled with rage.

At about 8pm the battalion settled down for the evening to try and get what rest they could.

Reveille the following day was at 5am. The men breakfasted and managed to have a welcome wash and shave. Second-Lieut Burroughes was sent on a reconnoitring patrol with three men to see how far the battalion could move forward. His patrol managed to follow a path for about 1200 yards before being fired on by Turkish soldiers. The battalion's watering hole was temporarily interdicted by the Medical Officer, forcing the battalion to get their water from a well close to the enemy's line and under continuous shell fire. Eight men at a time were sent out, only one man to collect the water while the other seven gave him covering fire. Due to a disparity in numbers within the different companies, they were reorganised to try and balance the number of men in each. This was not a popular decision: many of the men had enlisted together at the beginning of the war, they had trained together and grown to rely on each other. Now at the moment when they felt they would need each others' support they were being separated.

At 2pm acting Sergt-Major Wells reported and informed the Colonel that the battalion had to be ready to attack at 4pm that day. They were to clear snipers out of the valley to the front of the battalion's position, join up with the 53rd Division on the right and the 10th on the left and dig in for the night ready for the main attack the following day. The Norfolks were on the right of the line, the Hampshires in the centre and the Suffolks on the left. The battalion was to move forward single file in snake formation. As the Norfolks prepared for battle we can only surmise what must have been going through their minds as the hour of attack drew closer. Although patriotic and keen these men were also woefully inexperienced. They had not had time to acclimatise to the harsh Turkish climate nor to get used to battle-field conditions. Most had never faced a real enemy before, and the enemy they were about to attack was both professional and committed. The Turks were determined to protect their country whatever the cost, and considered the European invaders as infidels determined to destroy the Moslem people and change their way of life. The Norfolks' assault on the Turkish positions was not one of the greatest attacks of the First World War but it was without doubt to be one of the most infamous.

Chapter seven

The Battle

No mother or father saw him die,
No sister or brother to say goodbye
No friends or relations to grasp his hand
But they hope to meet in the better land.

Personal Column
Morning Post 1914

From the beginning the attack was totally confused. The orders came so quickly that the battalion hardly had time to prepare. Lance-Corp Thrower was making tea with some friends when Capt Pattrick came running up and told them to prepare for an attack. The men acted quickly, putting on their cartridge belts, grabbing their rifles and running to their front-line positions. A number of officers and men expressed concern about attacking in broad daylight over unfamiliar ground with little cover, but these concerns appear to have been ignored.

The Norfolks' orders do not appear to have been very clear. Most of the officers seemed to think that their orders were to attack the area in front of their position and clear it of Turkish snipers and machine-gun positions in readiness for the main British attack the following day. Others thought the objective was to clear and capture the village of Anafarta Saga on the Tekke Teppe ridge. Whatever their orders, preparations for the attack were poor. They had no idea of the position of their Brigade Headquarters, the field-dressing stations, the reserve ammunition, or even where to locate the battalion's machine guns.

Despite this however, at approximately 4.15pm on 12 August 1915 the Norfolks left their trenches and attacked towards the Turkish lines. The mystery surrounding the fate of the battalion during this attack became one of the legends of the First World War and it was Sir Ian Hamilton himself who, in his final despatches before being removed as Commander-in-Chief in Gallipoli, lent considerable weight to the mystery.

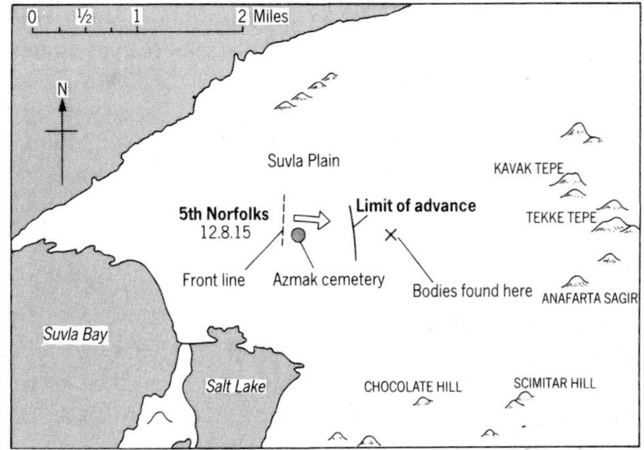

17. Map of the battlefield.

He wrote:

THE ARDENT NORFOLKS

In the course of the fight, creditable in all respects to the 163rd Brigade, there happened a very mysterious thing. The 1/5th Norfolks were on the right of the line, and found themselves for a moment less strongly opposed than the rest of the brigade. Against the yielding force of the enemy Colonel Sir H. Beauchamp, a bold, self confident officer, eagerly pressed forward, followed by the best part of the battalion. The fighting grew hotter, and the ground became more wooded and broken. At this stage many men were wounded or grew exhausted with thirst. These found their way back to camp during the night. But the Colonel, with sixteen officers and 250 men, still kept pushing on, driving the enemy before him. Amongst these ardent souls was part of a fine company enlisted from the King's Sandringham estates. Nothing more was ever seen or heard of any of them. They charged into the

> forest, and were lost to sight or sound. Not one of them ever came back.

The truth is not quite as mysterious as Sir Ian Hamilton would have us believe. The attacking line consisted of the 5th Norfolks to the right, the 8th Hampshires in the centre and the 5th Suffolks on the left. The 4th Norfolks, which had been left behind at Suvla Bay during the initial landing to unload stores, was moved up into the brigade's support trenches. As the men prepared for action their commanding officer Colonel Beauchamp sent a message to the battalion: 'Now then 5th Norfolks go and do your best; the General is behind to see.'

The officers, except the Colonel, dressed as soldiers and carried rifles in the hope that they would make less of a target for the Turkish snipers. Shortly before the attack was due to commence, Capt Ward, the battalion's adjutant, insisted that maps of the area be distributed to all the officers and NCOs, which delayed the attack by some fifteen minutes. Eight different maps of the peninsula were distributed, together with the battalion's picks and shovels. After receiving the maps the men discovered that none of them showed the area over which they had to attack, and most of the Company Commanders subsequently threw them away or shoved them into gorse bushes in disgust. Many of the Norfolks, who had been out in the Turkish sun all day, were already tired. One man, recognised as the battalion's chef, his water bottle empty, was already calling for water. The men had their collar buttons undone and their caps on back to front with wet khaki handkerchiefs inside to keep their heads cool. As the order to attack was received the first wave of men left the cover of their position and advanced towards the Turks, supported by the rapid fire of the reserve platoons. Sergt Walter Suddenham remembered the start of the attack: 'When the order to advance was given on 12 August the boys of the 5th Norfolks lined up ready for the attack just as they would on a field day. You would have thought we were back home on exercise.'

As well as to the officers, the younger soldiers looked to the more experienced men of the battalion, like Sergt Ernest Cranmer of D company, who had seen service against the Chins in India and the Boer Farmers during the South African campaign at the turn of the century. Much depended on NCOs like Sergt Cranmer if the attack by the 5th Norfolks was to succeed. Colonel Sir Horace Beauchamp and Capt Randall Cubitt led the attack. Both men were smoking, and the Colonel was waving his cane above his head as if he were on a British parade ground, spurring his men on and shouting his orders, 'On the Norfolks on, come on my holy boys, forward the hungry Ninth'; he was fearless. Capt Frank Beck strode ahead of the Sandringhams, stick in hand, his left leg and stick reaching the ground together as if he were back home in Norfolk walking across his beloved Sandringham estate. The men were encouraging each other with shouts of 'Come on Yarmouth' 'Good old Sandringham' 'Forward the Lynns' 'Come on Dereham show them the point'.

As the battalion moved forward they received orders to move half right. For some reason none of the other attacking battalions received this order and as the brigade advanced, a dangerous gap began to develop between the Norfolks and the rest of the attacking line. Major Purdy, seeing the danger, halted his company to allow the companies on the left of the line to come round and catch up but he was ordered to continue his advance by Brigadier Brusher. Capt Knight also saw the danger and tried to hold his company back but Colonel Beauchamp cursed him and ordered him to move and Capt Knight quickly lost touch with the rest of the battalion. Brigadier Brusher then ordered the battalion to fix bayonets and to advance at the double. These two orders given early in the attack when the men were at least a mile and a half from the Turkish positions did much to cause the disaster. The men were already totally exhausted by the time they reached the Turkish lines and too tired to make any form of rush at them. The battalion's bayonets shining in the sun not only told the Turkish troops that the attack had commenced but also gave away the battalion's position, making them an easy target for the Turkish gunners. Shell and shrapnel fire rained down onto the Norfolks from Turkish positions on Chocolate Hill. One shell fell among C company killing and wounding several men. The battalion quickly got themselves into artillery formation and despite the casualties pressed on.

They advanced in fifty-yard rushes, taking cover and resting whenever they could. They advanced through numerous small fields three to four acres in size surrounded by high fences, deep ditches and low, thick gnarled oaks with wide-spreading, dense leafy branches. After about a mile the battalion reached a small group of farm buildings. By this time they had come under heavy rifle and machine-gun fire from the front, the left and, more worryingly, the rear. The trees were full of well-concealed snipers and as the dust of battle grew thicker, visibility became limited to less than one hundred yards. As the heat and casualties began to take their toll, the Norfolks' attack started to flag. Due to the nature of the terrain with its deep ditches, dry water-courses, straggling hedges and thick gorse bushes, companies became separated, and began to lose cohesion. Heavy machine-gun and artillery fire had slowed the advance of both the 8th Hampshires and 5th Suffolks, but the Norfolks found themselves less strongly opposed and pressed on. As they did so they moved further away from any form of support the rest of the brigade may have been able to give. The battalion, now well in advance of the rest of the brigade, had left its rear totally exposed and the Turks began to surround them trying to cut off their line of retreat. Capt Montgomerie of the 4th Battalion of the Norfolk Regiment was watching the situation develop from the top of the hill overlooking the valley, from where he observed:

> It soon became apparent that the brigade was in difficulties. An officer of the 5th Suffolks came running back saying that the enemy was surrounding him. He said that the enemy were getting round their right flank. It then appeared to me that the enemy must be retreating across the front of the Hampshires and 5th Norfolks ... I, later, saw the brigade major, who told me they were having an awful time in front, and would probably have to retire ...

Lieut-Colonel Villiers Stuart, then a brigade major, was observing the area of the 5th Norfolks' attack through field glasses from the top of Kiretch Tepe. He had a good view of the battle, and later wrote.

> On the evening of 12 August 1915, I was observing the low ground in the neighbourhood of Anafarta Ova through field glasses from the top of Kiretch Tepe Ridge, a distance of about 2000 to 2500 yards, when, to my surprise I saw what appeared to be about a battalion of our troops advancing rapidly, and apparently unsupported towards the enemy positions on Kavak Tepe. Knowing that there was a considerable

concentration of Turks in a gully south-east of Kidney Hill on the left flank of the advance, I anticipated trouble and got the two mountain guns attached to my brigade (30th), ready for action to try to protect the left flank of the advancing troops. Almost immediately the Turks debouched from their cover and attacked our men in the flank and rear.

It was soon too dark to see the issue of the fight, but at the time I was afraid they would be destroyed.

Major Villiers Stuart's observations were quite right, and as casualties began to mount, the 5th Norfolks became involved in a desperate struggle against the Turks for their very existence. The trees seemed to be alive with snipers, most of them painted green, including their rifles, and disguised with branches, twigs and leaves tied around their bodies. Many were later captured and several turned out to be sixteen-year-old girls. Due to the heat physical exhaustion began to take its toll and men began to drop out. Corp Johnson collapsed, his clothes soaked with perspiration. Fortunately Capt Fawkes, his company commander, saw him and gave him some brandy telling him to get back the best way he could. Capt Fawkes then continued with the attack. Casualties began to mount and from the various accounts of survivors we can establish what befell many of the battalion. Private Dawson of A company was by the side of Capt Mason, his company commander, when Mason was shot through the leg and wounded, Private Brown of the same company helped Mason to his feet. The Captain insisted on staying with his men and a short time later he was shot in the head and killed. Private Medlock remembered how heavy the fighting got, in a letter home to his brother. He was also one of the last people to see Capt Randall Cubitt:

We found ourselves eventually in a vineyard, a sort of triangular bit of ground and not a very big place. Here we took shelter, about a dozen of us. Other men came in and joined us, including Sergt Allen. Some of the men went through a gap in the vineyard and what became of them I don't know, but I should almost think they were shot down. I don't know whether there were or were not all Norfolks, but the officer that went through with them was Capt Randall Cubitt.

The next person to see Capt Cubitt was Private Dawson and he later recollected the incident:

> Capt Cubitt came over the trench side through a hedge revolver in hand he ran up to me and said 'You watch out for the Turks as they come around the corner of the trench.' Two minutes later I was shot through the foot. I turned to speak to Captain Cubitt when I saw him laying dead on his back, I put my hand on his head to make sure he was dead and then crawled away.

Private Tubby of the Yarmouth company charged forward shouting 'Come on Yarmouth', and was immediately shot and killed. Major Woodwark was seen advancing at the head of his men when he suddenly threw his hands above his head and fell backwards, shot and killed by a sniper. Private Alfred Pearson of the Lynn Company, who was lying wounded by some rocks, saw his company commander Capt Pattrick, together with Sergt Ernest Beart, surrounded by Turkish soldiers. Capt Pattrick had been wounded in the leg and was bleeding profusely. The Turkish soldiers took their weapons and marched them away as prisoners-of-war, but neither man was ever seen again. Second-Lieut Randall Burroughes was seen to fall at the head of his men as he encouraged them on. He was nineteen years old. (His young brother Stephen, who was an officer with the Kings Royal Rifle Corps, was killed in France during the last few days of the war, thereby destroying the future of the Burroughes family.) Second-Lieut Marcus Oliphant climbed to the top of a ditch and was shot in the chest. Private Tom Williamson ran to his side and noticed that a bullet had passed straight through Oliphant's body. He covered the wounds as best he could with a field dressing. Oliphant ordered him to take command of the platoon and continue with the attack, he was finished. Second-Lieut Marcus Oliphant was never seen again. A friend was later to write to his father:

> I can see him now, patient in pain, calm in the disorder and insisting that he was quite all right, when almost done. Great, noble, pure and heroic! I go ahead and thank God that I could have known such a splendid soul.

Although clearly suffering from fatigue, Capt Frank Beck was seen still leading the Sandringhams about a mile from their starting position. He had his hat in one hand and his revolver in the other.

A shell was then seen to explode quite close to him and he disappeared from sight. He was later seen by Private Dye sitting under a tree, his head to one side. Dye was unable to say whether he was dead, wounded or just totally exhausted. Captain Coxon ran into a small farm at the head of his men and was shot in the throat. Bugler Swan, who was just behind the Captain, leapt over a wall into the yard of the farm but was also shot in the throat before he had time to take cover. Both men, now badly wounded and in great pain, tried to crawl back to the British lines, but were surrounded and captured by the Turks within sight of their own lines. As Scout Wilfred Ellett from Yarmouth stumbled over the rough ground a Turkish sniper shot him in his left foot. He managed to crawl to a small farm cottage close by to take cover. Once inside he noticed a Turkish sniper lying across the rafters in the roof of the cottage. Before the sniper had time to react, Ellett managed to shoot him and he fell to the floor, and that, as Ellett put it, 'was the end of his day's work'. Sergt Tubbenham was ordered to return to the beach for reinforcements but he had not gone far when a sniper started taking shots at him. He took cover behind a rock and started to return the fire but was shot in the foot by yet another unseen Turkish soldier. As he started to crawl away from the area, the snipers still taking pot shots at him, he spotted a stretcher bearer but as he approached him a shell exploded over-head and blew the man's eye out and Tubbenham ended up helping him back to the British lines. Private Herbert Saul, who disliked carrying a rifle and hated the killing and misery of war had enlisted only on the condition that he could be a stretcher-bearer and not carry arms. Time and time again during the battle 'Old Saul', as he was affectionately called by the troops, went out under the most murderous fire to rescue the wounded. They say he had a charmed life; the men he had already rescued begged him not to go out again as his luck must run out. 'Its all right', he would reply in his deep Norfolk voice, 'they can't hit me – they haven't done so yet.' He was promoted to the rank of sergeant on the field for his bravery. Fourteen-year-old Private George Carr had become totally exhausted; fortunately for him he was close to Old Saul, who managed to get him off the battle field and to the safety of a dressing station. Private Cliff Harrison was lying on the ground firing towards the Turkish positions when a shell exploded close to him, shrapnel hit him in the face and blinded him. To add to the

Norfolks' difficulties, part of a relieving force began to fire on them thinking they were Turks. A signaller named Jarvis snatched up some flags and jumping to the top of the trench, and under a hail of fire from both the British and Turkish positions, succeeded in signalling a message to the British position and they stopped firing.

Nineteen-year-old Private Albert Francis of D company had one of the luckiest escapes when a sniper's bullet entered his tunic, took a piece out of his belt and severed his lanyard before passing through his left arm. Private Julian Lockwood was hit in the head by a piece of shrapnel and fell to the floor. When he recovered he found that not only was he still under fire but that his rifle, bayonet and ammunition were gone. He managed to crawl into a ditch and take cover until some stretcher bearers found him and carried him to the beach. As Sergt Thomas Jakeman, one of the battalion's drill instructors, advanced next to Second-Lieut Beauchamp, whose side he had been at throughout the attack, he was shot in the arm and knocked backwards. As Jakeman tried to get up he was shot again, this time in the thigh. Lieut Beauchamp turned to Jakeman and said, 'I'm very sorry Jakeman, but we must go through with it.' Beauchamp then vanished into one of the small farms that were scattered everywhere, and was never seen again. Second-Lieut Robert Adams, who had joined the battalion together with his friend Alec Beck, was last seen chasing some Turkish soldiers along a trench in company with some of his men. He and his men then vanished from sight. Lance-Corp Beales was taking cover in one of the many ditches when he saw Capt Trevor Oliphant get hit and fall. Corp Beales climbed out of his ditch and in full view of the enemy and under heavy fire ran two hundred yards to drag the wounded officer to cover. On his way back he heard a cry for help and found a wounded soldier of the Hampshire Regiment laying in a gorse bush. He ran to the rear of his own position, collected some stretcher bearers and had the man taken to safety, then returned to his own position and rallied his men ready for an expected Turkish counter-attack.

After advancing well into the plain and under constant fire Capt Knight finally found Lieut Birkbeck's platoon and ordered them to withdraw. He then found Sergt John Goulder who informed him that the rest of the battalion was considerably to the left. Capt Knight, leaving one platoon behind to watch his flank, advanced with the rest of his men until they came to a farm building. They

18. Second-Lieutenant Rollo Pelly.

managed to rush it, bayoneting the five or six Turks hidden inside. Knight and his men became pinned down by heavy Turkish machine-gun fire, about fifty yards to the front of their position. While Capt Knight, Major Barton and Sergt Goulder were discussing their next step Sergt Goulder was shot in the head and killed by a sniper who had concealed himself up a tree. Capt Knight managed to spot the Turk, grabbed Goulder's rifle and managed to shoot him before slowly withdrawing his men from the building.

Second-Lieut Pelly was shot in the face and seriously wounded. He later wrote in his diary:

> It only felt like a jab from a needle and I carried on till one of my men saw me and said 'Oh Lord, it's our officer.' At this I put my hand up to my face and found a sea of blood. The bullet had broken both sides of my lower jaw shredded my tongue and blown my teeth out through the right cheek leaving my chin hanging by the skin on my chest.

He was finally patched up by two members of the Royal Army Medical Corps, who carried him on a stretcher through the scrub and under fire for several miles back to the beach. He later wrote of his first experiences of battle in a letter to his parents:

> I didn't have many feelings under fire, it was all so sudden. It never entered my head to run away but did to take jolly good cover and stop and get my breath whenever possible. When we were right in the thick of it I think my thoughts were somewhat thus: O God, if I can be of any use use me but if not bring on the darkness mighty quick! I saw no man run away.

Such was the confusion after the battle that for several days Pelly was thought to have been killed. It wasn't until someone spotted him in a casualty clearing station some days later that they realised that he had survived.

Major Purdy meanwhile was organising a bayonet charge with Capt Ward to clear some trenches of Turkish soldiers. As they charged forward Major Purdy was shot in the arm and was knocked to the ground. He lay still for some minutes with bullets zipping all round him, then tried to get up but was shot again, this time in the side, and fell back. Now in great pain Major Purdy began to crawl his way back to his own lines, his left arm completely useless and blood pouring from his side. He managed to take cover in a narrow ditch where he met another Norfolk whom he described as 'a skulker' keeping his head down. This man helped dress Major Purdy's wounds before trying to steal his watch and making off. Major Purdy then continued to walk back towards the rear to get medical attention. On his way he heard a wounded man calling out for help in a nearby field and went to assist. He discovered it was an Australian soldier with two bullet wounds in his stomach. What an Australian was doing in the middle of a British attack Major Purdy was unable to discover. He gave him some water and covered his wounds with iodine, then found some stretcher bearers and ordered them to remove the Australian to a field hospital. The Turkish army was now counter-attacking from the hills on the left and the air was alive with bullets. As he continued Major Purdy found a group of eight Norfolks taking cover in a ditch. Amongst them was the platoon commander, Corpl Darby, who had a bullet in the stomach and was in great pain, and Corpl Green of B company, with a bullet through the lower part of his throat. Corpl Green said he was not in pain, in fact had no sensation at all in the lower part of his body. Both men looked very weak and Purdy gave them both some brandy. Corpl Darby survived the battle; alas, poor Green did not. Major Purdy then came across the adjutant of the Suffolks who made him lie down and took his equipment off. As Major Purdy lay there Capt Knight of the Sandringham company came running up asking for reinforcements. He had been with Lieut Birbeck, who was to the right of their position and was holding out against overwhelming numbers of Turkish soldiers but was being hard pressed by them. Lawrence was unable to spare any men and suggested that Knight should go back to Brigade Headquarters, outline how desperate their position had become and try to bring up reinforcements from there. Capt Knight set off. Later this action was to be seen by some, unfairly, as an act of cowardice. Sir Dighton Probyn, comptroller of Queen Alexandra's household, never spoke to him again. Finally Major Purdy made his way in great pain to the field hospital where he was treated and later evacuated on a hospital ship.

Capt Culme-Seymore, the battalion's machine-gun officer, probably had the most confusing battle. On commencing the attack the Commanding Officer Colonel Beauchamp told him to move his machine guns with the reserve company. While he was getting into position, Major Kennedy, the divisional staff officer, told him to get his guns to the front line so he moved them up. He had no mules, and the ammunition and everything else had to be carried by hand. When he arrived at the front line Colonel Beauchamp, ordered him in a wrath back to the reserve. However Kennedy was still there so Capt Culme-Seymore halted the guns in front of the reserve. By now his machine-gun company were taking casualties and he was left with only four men to carry two guns, their tripods and ammunition. The only way the company could move this much equipment

19. *Officers of the 1st/5th Bn. The Norfolk Regiment:*
Back row (standing) left to right: Lt. T. Oliphant, (wounded 12.8.15), Lt. V.M. Cubitt (killed in action 12.8.15), *Lt. G.W. Birkbeck,* (killed in action 19.4.17), *2nd Lt. M.B.G. Proctor-Beauchamp* (killed in action 12.8.15), *2nd Lt. A.G. Culme-Seymour, Capt. A.H. Mason* (killed 21.8.15), *Lt. A.E.A. Beck* (killed in action 12.8.15), *Capt E. Gay* (killed in action 12.8.15), *Capt A.C.M. Coxon,* (prisoner-of-war 12.8.15), *Maj. E.R. Woodwark* (killed in action 21.8.15), *2nd Lt. M.F. Oliphant* (killed in action 12.8.15), *Capt. F.R. Beck* (killed in action 12.8.15).
Middle row (seated) l to r: Capt. E.R. Cubitt (killed in action 12.8.15), *Capt. A.D. Pattrick* (killed in action 12.8.15), *Maj. W.J. Barton, Lt. Col. Sir H.G. Proctor-Beauchamp* (killed in action 12.8.15), *Capt. and Adj. A.E.M. Ward* (killed in action 12.8.15), *Capt. A. Knight,* (wounded 12.8.15).
Front row l to r: 2nd Lt. W.G.S. Fawkes (prisoner-of-war 12.8.15), *2nd Lt. W. James, 2nd Lt. S.C. Larn, 2nd Lt. M.B. Buxton, 2nd Lt. A.R. Pelly* (wounded 12.8.15).

by hand was to carry part of it about one hundred yards and then run back for the rest. Finally the heat and exertion overcame Capt Culme-Seymore and he collapsed completely exhausted and was carried off the field on a stretcher.

Despite the desperate casualties Colonel Beauchamp, with 250 officers and men, continued to advance through a wood towards the Turkish positions. The Colonel was last seen arm-in-arm with Capt Ward inside a farm on the other side of the wood. His last known order was, 'Now boys, we've got the village. Let's hold it.' This wood was then set alight, whether as a result of shelling or a deliberate tactic by the Turks in order to cut the battalion off we will never be sure. What is true is that most of the men that followed Colonel Beauchamp were never seen again. The remainder of the battalion was stopped from entering the wood by Evelyn Beck who had seen the danger as the Turks began to encircle Colonel Beauchamp and his men. They held out until the early hours of the following morning, before being relieved by the Essex Regiment. It had been a disaster, of that there was little doubt; but what had befallen those in the battalion who entered the wood? Speculation was to continue for over seventy- five years: the legend of the Vanished Battalion was born.

Chapter eight

The Aftermath

Here dead lie we because we choose not
To live and shame the land from which we sprung.
Life, to be sure, is nothing much to lose;
But young men think it is, and we were young.
A.E. HOUSMAN (1859-1936)

News of the battalion's fate emerged slowly. The day following the battle, 13 August, a hospital ship containing about forty wounded Norfolks sailed first to Imbros and then onto Malta, arriving on the 17th. Major Purdy, anxious for news of the battalion, searched the ship for his men. From number one platoon he found Coleman, Bullock, Strong, Keeler and Bircham, from number two platoon Pawley, Busby, Spurling, Allison, Tooke and Smalley and from three and four platoon, Dawson, Francis, Marjoram, Medlock and Meggett. He also discovered that his friend Sergt Goulder had been killed, as had Capt Mason and Capt Randall Cubitt. After arriving in Malta the men were transferred to St Andrews Hospital. The hospital stood on top of a hill north west of Schliema; it was fairly new, about ten years old, and more importantly, almost free of flies. It must have seemed like heaven after the conditions they had had to endure in Gallipoli. Purdy teamed up with Capt Culme-Seymour and between them they became friendly with a good few Australian and New Zealand officers. The senior chaplain of the 53rd Division, Davies, was also there. Purdy found Davies to be a remarkable man. He wrote letters for those who could not write, found writing paper for those who could, produced cigarettes from 'thin air' for the patients, found books, and visited every man in the hospital (800 of them) at least once a day. On 20 August Major Purdy was embarked onto the P&O ship *Somali* and enjoyed a pleasant voyage home. It was only upon his return that he was to discover the full extent of the losses incurred by the battalion.

Second-Lieut Pelly found himself on the same hospital ship as Major Purdy. He was the last patient aboard and was extremely lucky to make it. He was unable to speak and very weak from loss of blood; eating consisted of sucking milk down a tube and even this was quite painful. The doctors decided not to set his smashed jaw until he was stronger. Saliva and some blood poured from Pelly's mouth and flies became a great nuisance. He was taken to Tignes Hospital, where he remained for three weeks. His main problem was how to take sustenance, as anything poured down his mouth flooded down his neck, choking him. A young nurse came to the rescue by devising a rubber tube attached to an enamel funnel into which she poured egg flips, the flow of which Pelly controlled by pinching the tube. On arrival in England he was sent to the Lady Evelyn Mason's private hospital, where he endured five major operations to repair his jaw. On Christmas Eve 1915 Second-Lieut Rolland Pelly finally drank tea out of a cup, after many months he was on the mend.

As none of the men who took part in the attack were reported killed, only missing, the relatives were left in an agony of suspense. The papers were alive with speculation. The Mayor of King's Lynn, Mr Ridley, received a letter regarding prisoners-of-war from Colonel Woodwark of the Royal Army Medical Corps, the brother of Major Ernest Reginald Woodwark of the 5th Battalion:

> On Saturday last we heard by telegram from the Embassy at Constantinople that it is greatly hampered in communicating with the prisoners in Constantinople, Angora and Afron-Kara Hissar, so you ought not to feel discouraged if a reply is slow in reaching you. The Embassy have already reported that over 400 prisoners are known to be in Turkish hands and this number is far in excess of names of prisoners of war hitherto returned. The Turks are very slow in answering official enquiries forwarded by the Embassy.

This letter raised the hopes of the families of the missing men, but their hopes were to be quickly dashed.

The first definite news came from one of the medical officers attached to the Welsh division who had been involved in the fighting on the right of the 5th Norfolks. He reported that at about 8pm on 12 August, eighteen men of the 5th Norfolks crawled into his dressing station with the most fearful bayonet wounds he ever

THE GALLANT 5th NORFOLKS

65 OF THE YARMOUTH MEN IN THE DARDANELLES.

Lce Cpl. A. T[illegible] (missing).

Lce Cpl. H. F. Leggett (missing).

Pte. A. Durrant (missing).

Scout J. C. Bushell (missing).

Pte. Reginald Bl[illegible] (missing).

Sergt. G. Cleveland (killed August 13th 1915).

Pte. C. Millican (in hospital).

Pte. W. Groom (missing).

Pte. S. Grice.

Co.-Sergt.-Maj. B. Parker (wounded).

Pte. Robert Denton, 4th Norfolks (wounded).

Pte. Arthur Parker.

Pte. Ernest G. Parker

Pte. Bert Reyner.

Pte. Wm. Moss (invalided home).

Bugler P. Pearce (wounded).

Sig. A. Hellenburgh (missing).

Pte. C. Moseley.

Corpl. G. Catchpole.

Sergt. A. Rivett.

20. *Newspaper report in the* Yarmouth Mercury
16 October 1915.

TE. H. G. HACON (missing).
CORPL. S. BRACEY (missing).
PTE. C. H. WESTGATE (missing).
PTE. F. G. BECKETT (missing).
PTE. S. BOWLES (missing).

. FRED. C. SAVILLE.
PTE. STANLEY SMITH.
PTE. W. DAVEY.
PTE. V. C. BUCKINGHAM.
PTE. SIDNEY BAKER.

E. H. E. DARNELL (wounded).
PTE. F. R. LYNES (wounded).
PTE. A. ROUSE (killed August 25th 1915).
PTE. G. A. BROWNE (wounded).
PTE. T. DODSON (missing).

TE. L. FULLER.
PTE. A. PALMER.
PTE. H. ALLENBURY.
PTE. LAYTON.
PTE. A. J. MARJORAM.

W. J. SEAMAN.
PTE. W. KEMP.
PTE. M. HARBORD.
PTE. W. L. JAYE.
SCOUT W. ELLETT
LCE.-CPL. A. HOWES.

saw. He dressed them and sent them on stretchers to the hospital. He further stated that, as a doctor, he was sure not one of them would live twenty-four hours. The men had told him that their company had become isolated in one of the big gullies. When they entered apparently no one was about, but suddenly thousands of Turkish soldiers surrounded them and shot them at close range, so close, the doctor said, that powder was in all the wounds, which were cauterised. A hand-to-hand bayonet scrap followed and these eighteen said they were the only ones who cut themselves out. All the rest, they were sure, were killed.

Corporal Blott of the 5th Norfolks wrote home to his mother in Norfolk describing the battle:

> It was just a jumbled-up affair. The hills were alive with rifles and machine guns but still we went rushing forward. As they fell on the enemy NCOs were shouting to cheer the men up, but there was not any need for that for they fought like devils let loose.

Eustace Cubitt wrote home to his parents at Honing Hall:

> 17th August 1915
>
> My dear Father,
>
> By the time this letter reaches you, you will probably have heard about our poor regiment. We went into action last Wednesday and got it frightfully hot. But news of the officers and men missing is so vague. I dare not venture to speculate as to the fate of those who are not with us now. Our numbers as we stand at present are about 400 men and alas only six officers, Major Barton, Gervase, Evelyn Beck, Murray Buxton, James and myself. A large number of officers are missing including Randall and Victor, but as so many officers that all went into action together are missing we all have strong hopes that they are prisoners ... I am told that prisoners are treated well especially officers so don't worry as there is quite a good possibility that they are all right ...
>
> Yours very affectionately
>
> Eustace

Capt Evelyn Beck, who had stopped his men entering the burning wood and thereby probably saved their lives, wrote to Frank Beck's brother Arthur at the estate office on the Sandringham estate.

> 25 August 1915
>
> We were suddenly told we had to make an advance that afternoon at four o'clock. This we did and came under a very heavy shell fire as soon as we left our position. Anyway we kept on with the attack. I am sorry to say it was not a success, the battalion was cut up very badly indeed. I think there were many more Turks in front than was supposed. We had to advance across a piece of country very much what our farm looked like when we took it over, but much smaller fields and no end of little stone farm houses about every hundred acres. The fields had very high hedges and deep ditches round them. This caused our men to get into small parties and the Turks knowing the country cut us up awfully. Out of the whole battalion we had left 384 men and four officers, Major Barton, Birkbeck, one Cubitt [Eustace] and myself. Where the others are all gone no one knows. Some must be killed but I cannot believe all and I think they must have been taken prisoner. The last I saw of Alec and Uncle Frank they were just one field behind me. At least Alec was going strong Uncle Frank was more on my right. I went on until the Turkish fire and machine guns held us up when we opened fire on them until dark. I found myself with about forty men of the Norfolks and four other regiments. At about nine o'clock the Turks worked round on my left flank and killed some more. Then the beggers set the corn and grass on fire in the fields in front and drove us out. I then took up another position further back. Then they worked round my right and enfiladed me so I had to leave that and retire again until I came to the line the remnant of the brigade had taken up. Arrived at two o'clock Friday morning and dug ourselves in. In all there were about a 1000 men from nine different regiments. We held the line until relieved Sunday night by the Essex regiment which took our place … As we have not the list of wounded officers and men or prisoners at present I do hope and pray that old Alec and Uncle Frank may turn up all right. At present it is impossible to find out anything.

The first positive news about the fate of the Sandringhams came from Private Tom Williamson of F company. He had seen the remnants of the company making a last stand in a small farm house:

> The scrub seemed to be on fire all around us. The acrid smell surrounded us and the ground was hot through our boots. We continued to fire from the standing position but, as we proceeded, the line became uncontrollable as more and more blank spaces appeared when soldiers were shot or wounded. Then we saw the enemy. Somehow we had moved beyond our objective and were inside the enemy lines. Some of the Turks were actually behind us as we stood firing in the opposite direction. One by one the men of my section fell beside me. Then I was also shot through the right arm. It was as if I had been dealt a sudden, severe blow. My rifle fell to the ground.

Seeing that the rest of his section were all dead Williamson then began to make his way back towards the British lines when he came across the Sandringham Company.

> It was then that I passed by a farm and noticed that one company were sheltering there. I realized that this was the Sandringham Company … They were sheltering in a barn in a scrub-like area and the fires that I mentioned earlier had spread all around them. I saw the Sergeant of the Sandringham Company trying to rally his men around him. Many were already wounded and killed, and those who could not walk were destroyed by the fire, and others, who were actually inside the Turkish defences were out numbered and overpowered, and in any case were never heard of again.

The letters were followed by the inevitable telegrams. On 25 August 1915 Mrs Cubitt, Randall's wife, received the following:

> Regret to inform you that Captain E.R. Cubitt 5th Norfolk Regt is reported missing 12 August, this does not necessarily mean that he is killed or wounded.
> (Territorial Records, Warley)

As more and more of these telegrams were received by the families on the Sandringham estate, King George V became increasingly concerned about the fate of his estate workers. He personally cabled Sir Ian Hamilton for news of the battalion:

> I am most anxious to be informed as to the fate of the men of the 5th Battalion Norfolk Regiment as they include the

Sandringham Company and my agent Captain Frank Beck.
George RI

21. *His Royal Highness King George V with his Private Secretary, Stamfordham (Windsor Castle Royal Archives © 1992 Her Majesty the Queen).*

General Sir Ian Hamilton replied to the King on the 1st September 1915:

TO: H.M. King. Buckingham Palace London.

I greatly regret to inform Your Majesty that up to the present I have no news of the fate of the men of the 5th Norfolk Regiment beyond the fact that 14 Officers and about 250 men

> are missing including Sir H. Beauchamp the Commanding Officer and Capt F.R. Beck and Lieut A.Beck. General Inglefield reported to me personally that the battalion and their leaders were filled with ardour and dash and on coming into contact with the enemy pressed ahead of the rest of the Brigade into close broken country when he entirely lost touch of them and at the time could not tell me anything more. I have called for further information and will on receipt wire your majesty at once.
>
> Sir Ian Hamilton

On 2 September General Hamilton cabled Colonel Clive Wigram, assistant private secretary to the King:

> Late last night I got the King's cable asking about the Norfolk Regiment. I answered at once, giving him all the information I personally possessed, and cabling also to Inglefield, the Commander of the Division, to know what fresh information he possessed. The day after it happened I went out myself onto the ground to see Inglefield, and hear what I could about the extraordinary mischance. Some way short of the hills and in the plain, which is very wooded and broken into deep nullahs filled with long grass, trees, and all sorts of jungle, resistance was encountered. Sir H. Beauchamp who was, it seems, an extremely daring, adventurous person, pressed forward at a great pace, whereas the troops on his right hand and left hand seem to have been held up. Never, in any shape or form, could he get in touch with these fellows again. The rest of his line could not press on, and patrols he sent forward could not get through.

Sir Ian Hamilton cabled the King again on 3 September:

> General Inglefield can add nothing to the scanty details I was able to cable to Your Majesty on 1 September. Following is the state of Sandringham Company: missing Capt F.R. Beck, Lieut A. Beck. Wounded Capt A. Knight. Present Lieut A. E. Beck, of the 91 other ranks who landed at Suvla there are wounded 5, missing 21, sick in hospital 2, present 63.
>
> Sir Ian Hamilton

The King at once telegraphed the news to Frank Beck's brother Arthur, who was acting as his agent at Sandringham while Frank Beck was serving with the battalion.

> TO: Arthur Beck esq: Sandringham:
>
> I telegraphed to Sir Ian Hamilton for news of your brother and the Sandringham Company. In reply he says he is unable to ascertain any particulars except that their Brigadier reported that the Battalion and its leader on coming in contact with the enemy keenly dashed forward ahead of the Brigade into difficult country and entirely lost touch with the General. Further enquiries are being made on receipt of which I will at once let you know. I heartily sympathise with all the families who are left in suspense but I am proud that the Battalion has fought so splendidly.
>
> George RI

The national papers were soon full of the story:

> How the King's Servants Died at the Dardanelles
>
> Passing of the 'Ardent Souls' of Sandringham
>
> The Colonel who 'Still Pressed On'
>
> The Forest of Death and Why Norfolk Mournes
>
> The King's Message of Sympathy
>
> 'I am Proud they Fought so Splendidly'

The destruction of the 5th Norfolks and the battalion's close connections with the Royal Family made front-page news.

Letters were now also being received by the families of the rank and file who were still serving in Gallipoli. Private George Cann wrote home to his parents in Yarmouth:

> We have returned from the trenches again for a short spell. You would laugh to see us, for we look more like Turks, black and bearded. Mr Saul says I look fine in mine. He has been

> promoted sergeant in the stretcher bearers as the doctor has been wounded. He has done good work out here, and deserves a VC. George Cleveland was killed about a week ago, and several other Yarmouth and Gorleston men have followed him. We lost about fifty per cent of our battalion due really to another big blunder. We went out during the advance too far and got surrounded, and had to make the best of our way back. When I think of it, it is really marvellous that any of us are still alive to-day ... Do you know where Alf is yet? [Alf Cann, was killed when HMS *The Royal Edward* was sunk by a German submarine on its way to Gallipoli. Hundreds of men, many from Norfolk, went down with her. George would not have been aware of the loss.] It seems a terrible job here to get food and water in the trenches. We were two days without anything to eat, and often had but half a cup of water a day ...

On 17 August Private Leslie Jay of D company wrote to his parents:

> Just a line to let you know I am quite well and safe. It is awfully hot here and with the fighting we get a fairly warm time of it ... I shall be glad when it is all over, which I hope will not be long.

On 20 August he wrote again:

> It is awfully hot and dry, but the sea here is beautifully warm and we often bathe under shell fire. Things have been rather warm here for the last day or two and they have given us plenty of shrapnel, which we certainly cannot call pleasant ...

Other letters began to reveal for the first time the fate of some of the missing soldiers. Private Joseph Bentley was only nineteen years old. He had joined the 5th Battalion at the outbreak of war and as the youngest member of B company was extremely popular with the older soldiers. Corp Foster of the same company wrote to Bentley's parents:

> You will no doubt have seen by the papers that our battalion has been in action, and unfortunately we have not come out of the ordeal without some casualties, and it is with the greatest regret and sorrow that I have to tell you that Joe was killed. He at the time was fighting side by side with Jack and a piece of

> shell hit him in the head. I can not possibly describe my feelings as I give you this sad news, but trust that you will find room in your hearts to forgive me for breaking the news to you.

Other letters and stories had the strangest of twists. Sergt Matthews of the C company of the 5th Battalion the Royal Welsh Fusiliers had gone out into no man's land a few days after the battle to try to 'bag some Turkish snipers'. He had some success. On searching their bodies, as well as finding hundreds of British identity disks he discovered a letter addressed to a young woman in Peterborough from a Private W. Frost of the 5th Norfolks. Sergt Matthews wrote to the woman:

> Dear Miss Thorpe,
>
> You will be surprised to have a letter from a stranger but I though it my painful duty to write this letter. On 21 August I and three of my men were sent out after Turkish snipers and I was lucky enough to get one and had to shoot him. After searching him to try and get any information like trench maps in his pockets, I found your letter which you sent to your young man who must have been shot by this sniper. I thought you might like to know that we have avenged your lovers death.
>
> I remain yours
>
> Sergt Matthews C company A platoon
>
> 1.5th Royal Welsh Fusiliers

Miss Thorpe replied at once thanking Sergt Matthews for his kind letter but also informing him that in fact Private Frost although badly wounded and having all his personal effects looted had been found alive and was now recovering well in an Alexandra hospital.

Some while after the battle Sergt Cowles wrote to his parents informing them that with the exception of a slight graze to his hand caused by a bullet and a swollen knee, he was quite fit and well. This letter came as quite a shock to them as they had been informed some days before that he had in fact been killed in action; Sergt Cowles survived the war.

A letter was then delivered to the wife of Private Arthur Thomas Webber of the Yarmouth Company of the 5th Norfolks informing her that he had been taken prisoner-of-war. This news came as a bit of a shock to Private Webber's wife as she had been drawing her widow's pension for some weeks. Further hopes that more men may have been taken prisoner were raised. A postcard was received by Mrs Coxon, the mother of Capt Cedric Coxon, stating that although he was wounded, the bullet had missed his carotid artery. Trying to get back to the British lines he had been taken prisoner only a few hundred yards from safety. He had made a nine-day cart trip over

22. *Prisoners-of-war in Constantinople:* (second from left, sitting) *Captain Coxon,* (fourth from left, sitting) *Captain Fawkes (Liddle Colection).*

Turkish mountains to Constantinople where he was now a prisoner-of-war; he was well and was being treated properly. Further news was then received that Capt Fawkes was also a prisoner in Constantinople. Mrs Blott, the mother of Private William Blott, received a letter from her son:

> Just a few lines to let you know that I am a prisoner of war in Turkey and that I am quite well, and am being well treated. I have had a very exciting time this last month and this is the first chance I have had of writing to you. I know you must have been worrying. I may not write much to you, but will write when I can, only don't worry if you don't get a letter.

As well as the two officers twelve other ranks were also found to have been taken prisoner. Further news was received by Sir Ian Hamilton, who cabled King George.

> A Turkish prisoner has said that he saw seventy British prisoners near Bulair a few days ago so these *might* be some of the Norfolks.

In the House of Commons Sir Robert Price, MP asked the Under-secretary of State for War whether he had any information about the number of men of the 5th Norfolks missing since 12 August and whether it was now possible to state whether any, and which of them, were prisoners-of-war.

Mr Tennant replied:

> Of about 200 men reported missing up to date only seven have been reported to the War Office as prisoners-of-war. It is possible that some of the others who are recorded as missing may be in direct communication with their relatives, but I cannot give any figure for these men. Every effort has been made to obtain from the Turkish Government full lists of the Prisoners of War in their hands, but so far these efforts have not been successful.

This was followed by a letter from General Braithwaite, Chief of the General Staff, marked *Strictly private and confidential*, stating that they now had knowledge that a number of prisoners had been taken and were in captivity in Constantinople.

The news heartened Queen Alexandra and she got her friend, General Sir Dighton Probyn V.C., to make enquiries with the American Embassy in Constantinople for news of the Sandringham Men.

His Excellency.
The Hon: Walter H.Page.
U.S. Embassy.
October 27th 1915.

Dear Mr Page,

I write by direction of Queen Alexandra to beg of Your Excellency's assistance in a matter in which Her Majesty is deeply interested.

There is a certain Captain F.R.Beck, for whom Her Majesty has a very great regard, having known him personally for some 50 years – ever since his childhood.

For considerably over 20 years he has been Agent at Sandringham, having succeeded his father in that Office. Long before the war broke out he, at the suggestion of King Edward, who was anxious to help the Territorial movement, raised a Company of men on the Sandringham Estate, and that company was eventually drafted into the 5th Norfolks ...

This regiment landed at Suvla Bay on the 9th of August last.

They went into action on the 12th of August, and from that day to this nothing has been heard of any of them ... For my part, having known Captain Beck intimately since his childhood, I never thought there was a chance of his being alive after I heard he was missing, as I felt he would be too gallant a man to surrender, and that he would only possibly have been induced to do so to save the lives of others, not his own. Now however on reading General Inglefield's despatch, and the cutting from local Norfolk papers, the hopes of Capt Beck's numerous friends and admirers have been raised, and amongst these sanguine people Queen Alexandra ranks the highest.

Her Majesty desires me to say she begs you kindly to do all you possibly can through your Embassy at Constantinople to ascertain if Captain F.R. Beck and his nephew, Lieut Alec Beck are amongst the prisoners there ...

I have taken upon myself to promise Queen Alexandra that Her Majesty may rest assured you will do all in your power to obtain for Her the information she is so anxious to get about her valued friend and servant.

I remain,

Dear Mr Page

At the beginning of December 1915 The Honourable Walter Page replied to Sir Dighton Probyn informing him that the Turkish Foreign Office could find no trace of either

23. *Her Majesty Queen Alexandra* (far right) *and Sir Dighton Probyn* (with white beard) *(Windsor Castle Royal Archives © Her Majesty the Queen).*

Frank or Alec Beck amongst the prisoners in Constantinople. They would of course inform Sir Dighton if any news of the men was received.

Hope was now fading. Sir Dighton thanked the American Ambassador for his help:

> If they are not Prisoners in that country, there can be no hope for them, and we must, I am afraid, feel certain they have been murdered, or at any rate given up their lives somewhere for their King and Country.

As time went on even the Royal Family began to loose hope. During a visit to Leeds to inspect military hospitals King George V met Private Arnold Doggett of the 5th Battalion, who had been wounded by shrapnel in both the back and neck. King George, pleased at seeing a member of the battalion, walked across to his bed, 'I see that you are a Norfolk man like myself, the best county no doubt'. Doggett thanked the King for his message of support just before the battalion left for the front. The King then enquired about the fate of the Sandringham Company and his agent Captain Beck. Doggett replied that he had probably been killed. The King looked depressed and replied that Doggett was probably correct.

It wasn't just the Royal Family that were making frantic enquiries to locate their friends and relatives. Lieut-Colonel Woodwark of the Royal Army Medical Corp, and brother of Major Woodwark of the 5th Norfolks, wrote letters to everyone and anyone and travelled the length and breadth of the country talking to survivors desperately trying to obtain information about his brother Ernest.

Mrs Pattrick, the wife of Capt Arthur Pattrick the Company Commander of the King's Lynn company, had some hope. Her husband had been seen taken prisoner-of-war by a member of his own company. Mrs Pattrick already had two children and was pregnant with her third. She turned to her brother-in-law for help and he contacted the Red Cross. Over the next few months the family received three letters from the Red Cross. The first was quite optimistic, the second a little more depressing and finally in December 1915 they received a letter which said: 'We regret that we can find absolutely no trace of Capt Arthur Pattrick in any Turkish hospital or POW camp'.

The news that both Randall and Victor Cubitt were missing as well as their cousin Randall Burroughes shattered the Cubitt family. Randall's wife was pregnant with their first child, who was born in the following October and named Thomas. His arrival helped a little to ease the pain of the loss of so many men from one family. Eustace, who survived the attack and was still in Gallipoli, made enquiries but was unable to trace his brothers. Enquiries were also made through the Red Cross for any further information but once again they were unable to find any trace of the missing men.

Despite this, messages kept appearing in the papers desperately seeking news of sons, husbands and fathers:

> Information Wanted
>
> L-Cpl Eassom
>
> Son of Mr and Mrs W. Eassom of Stribbington received notice on 20th September 1915 that their son is missing in the Dardanalles since 28 August 1915.
>
> Do any of his comrades have news or information about their missing son?

In 1916 the final telegrams from the Territorial Records Office in Warley began to arrive. Mrs Cubitt's arrived on 21 June 1916. It read:

> Dear Madam,
>
> The following notification has been received from the War Office today viz:- Capt E.R. Cubitt, 1/5th Batt'n. Norfolk Regiment. This Officer was reported missing 12 August 1915 on list No. M.3475. No further information has been received and in view of the lapse of time, his death has now been accepted for official purposes, as having occurred on or since 12th August 1915.
>
> With deepest sympathy, I am, Dear Madam

In January Mrs Cubitt received a letter from King George and Queen Mary expressing their deep sorrow at the loss of her husband in Gallipoli and assuring her that 'during the long months of uncertainty Their Majesties' thoughts had been constantly with her.'

Most of us can not possibly understand the grief felt by the family of nineteen-year-old Private Bentley but some of that grief came out a few days later when the following notice appeared in a local paper.

> BENTLEY – Joseph William, nineteen years, son of Mr and Mrs Bentley of 9 Saddlebow Road, Killed in action at the Dardanalles on 12 August.
>
> Although his hands I cannot clasp,
> His face I cannot see;
> Just let this little token tell
> That I remember thee.

It was not all doom and gloom. In January 1916 the *London Gazette* announced that both Alec and Evelyn Beck had been decorated with the Military Cross for outstanding bravery during the attack by the 5th Norfolks on 12 August 1915 (Alec Beck's award was, alas, a posthumous one), and Corp Beales was decorated with the Distinguished Conduct Medal. His citation read:

> For conspicuous gallantry during operations at Kuchuk Annafarta Ova, Gallipoli Peninsula, on 12 August 1915. He crawled out two hundred yards under heavy fire and brought in a wounded officer. Later he showed great coolness and presence of mind in assisting to rally the men of his platoon.

Thousands of men had been killed in Gallipoli, many from some of the most distinguished families in the land. Hundreds more had simply disappeared into the heat and dust of Turkish battle fields and were never to have a known grave. Yet despite this the stories about the fate of less than 200 men, the story of the missing Norfolks, would continue to cause speculation for three-quarters of a century.

Chapter nine

Corner of a Foreign Field

If I should die, think only this of me:
That there's some corner of a foreign field
That is forever England.

Rupert Brooke (1887-1915)

At the end of the war in November 1918 thousands of people whose friends and relatives were reported 'missing' became desperate for news of their loved ones. Thousands of people filed passed the tomb of the unknown warrior in the hope that it might be their son, husband or friend. The Cenotaph in London's Horse Guards Parade became the focus for British ceremonies of remembrance, while thousands of small memorials were built in every town, village and hamlet throughout the length and breadth of the land. These monuments drew those who knew private grief, and who, in their desperate effort to come to terms with their loss, sought to touch or run their fingers across the names of their loved ones engraved forever in stone.

The 'Lost Generation' of the 1914/18 war numbered over nine million killed, about one in eight of those who served; and most of these were under thirty years of age. Millions more were wounded, many suffering from the mental and physical scars of the Great War for the rest of their lives. These young men were also the very best each country had to offer: the strongest, the fittest, the brightest. Britain lost over 722,000 men, the cream of their generation. As Sir Winston Churchill later wrote, 'Too much blood had been spilt, too much life-essence consumed.'

In the nine months of bitter fighting during the Gallipoli campaign over 36,000 Commonwealth servicemen died. The thirty-one Commonwealth War Grave cemeteries on the peninsula contain 22,000 graves but it is only possible to identify 9,000 of these. The 13,000 who rest in unidentified graves in the cemeteries, together with the 14,000 whose remains were never found, are commemorated individually by name on the Helles

Memorial (British, Australian, and Indian names), the Lone Pine Memorial (Australian and New Zealand names), Twelve Tree Copse, Hill 60 and the Chunuk Bair Memorials (New Zealand).

Under the terms of the Armistice with Turkey the British Army re-entered the peninsula at the end of 1918 to clear the battle fields of hundreds of unburied bodies. This task was undertaken by the War Graves Commission and it was while carrying out this work that they made a startling discovery. A soldier making his way to a watering hole kicked up a Norfolks' regimental cap badge from under the sand. While searching for further souvenirs he suddenly came across the remains of a number of soldiers. He at once returned to his base and reported the find to his officer, who started

24. *The Reverend Charles Pierrepoint Edwards.*

an organised examination of the area, and sent for the Rev Charles Pierrepoint Edwards, MC, there on a special mission to try to establish what exactly had happened to the 5th Norfolks. It is this investigation that becomes central to the rest of the Vanished Battalion's story.

The Rev Pierrepoint Edwards was, to say the least, a very remarkable man. He was ordained deacon in 1887 and priest in 1888. He spent his first two years as a priest at St Giles Church, Colchester in Essex, followed by a further two years at North Woolwich, East London. It was while at this parish that he earned the nickname the 'fighting parson' for his staunch support of the Conservative party, especially during political meetings and marches when he was ready to defend his beliefs with both actions and words. In July 1898 he became the vicar of the island of West Mersea in Essex, a position he was to hold for almost the next fifty years, becoming affectionately known to the locals as 'Old Spiery'. In 1913 he joined the Territorial Army becoming chaplain to the 1/5 Suffolks, and immediately volunteered for foreign service. At the outbreak of the war he reported for duty and began training with the battalion. In July 1915 he sailed on the SS *Aquitaina* with the men of the East Anglian Division including the 5th Norfolks bound for Gallipoli. He landed with the brigade at Suvla Bay in August and moved inland with them. During the brigade's abortive attack on 12 August he remained in reserve but was to win the Military Cross for his bravery in going out into no-mans-land under heavy Turkish rifle and machine-gun fire to rescue wounded soldiers. His citation read:

> Reverend Edwards came around the Battalions of the 163rd Brigade, asking for volunteers to collect the wounded who had been out all night.
>
> Enemy snipers were busy and apparently treated all alike who came within their observation. But the gallant chaplain resolved to make an effort to bring in those poor fellows and a volunteer party of 24 men from the 5th Essex was soon made up and set out unarmed, with only stretchers and a large Red Cross flag.
>
> The General Officer Commanding the 163rd Brigade, afterwards wrote his thanks to the non commissioned officers and men who undertook this voluntary duty.

The Rev Edwards remained with the division in Gallipoli until he was evacuated in December 1915 on HMS *Victorian*. He spent a short time in Egypt, before returning to West Mersea where he remained for the rest of the war; 'Old Spiery' had done his bit.

The area where the badge had been found was cleared and close to where the remnants of the 5th Norfolks were last seen 180 bodies were discovered in a mass grave. One hundred and twenty-two of them were identified as men of the 5th Norfolks from their distinctive shoulder titles, the others were a mixture of the 5th Suffolks, the 8th Hants and a few men of the Cheshire Regiment. Only two were identifiable, those of Private Catter of the Suffolk Regiment and Private Barnaby of the Norfolks. Although the remains of three officers were discovered their identity discs were missing and it was impossible to identify them positively, although it is almost certain that one of them was Colonel Sir Horace Proctor Beauchamp because of his distinctive silver badges which were found with one of the bodies (he was the only officer in the battalion to wear his own badges). On 7 October 1919 the Norfolks' remains were given a Christian burial by the Rev Edwards in Azmak Cemetery, sharing their final resting place with 1074 other British and Commonwealth soldiers.

Soon the papers were full of the story; the *Irish Times* reported the finding of the bodies.

THE MISSING NORFOLKS

BODIES FOUND AT SUVLA

> After the lapse of nearly five years one of the greatest mysteries of the war has been solved. On the night of August 12th, 1915 during the fierce fighting which took place at Anafarta, on the Gallipoli Peninsula, when a battalion of the Norfolk Regiment disappeared. When the signal to advance was given Colonel Sir H. Beauchamp, with sixteen officers and 250 men pressed forward into a forest, driving the Turks before them. They never were seen again. In his despatch Sir Ian Hamilton alluded to the battalion's disappearance as 'a very mysterious affair' and there the matter rested until Wednesday when the Reverend C.S. Edwards, MC who has been employed in graves registration work on the Peninsula, presented a report to the War Office. He says that, on going

> over the Anafarta Plain, he found the remains of the missing men lying more than a mile beyond what had been the British front line. Apparently the battalion had advanced in perfect order and had been caught by a deadly hail of machinegun fire. 'Touching one another lay the bodies of fifty Britons and Turks, the heads of the latter facing seaward and those of the attackers towards their adversaries' lines'. The fate of the 5th Norfolks deserves to rank among the most glorious annals of our race. Cut off from help, they refused to surrender and died fighting. It was by spirit such as theirs that the war was won.

The Reverend Pierrepoint Edwards' official report, which remained a secret for over fifty years, however said nothing of glorious death, just of the horrors of war.

> What are almost certainly the remains of the officers and men of the 5th Norfolks who were missing after the action of the 12th August 1915 have now been discovered in a square 118.I. (Ref. 1/20000 Map.)
>
> The bodies were scattered over an area of about a square mile at an average distance of over 800 yards in rear of the Turkish front line and were lying most thickly round the ruins of a small farm. Up to date 180 bodies have been found, 122 of which have been identified by shoulder titles as belonging to the 5th Norfolks, such others as have been identified belong either to the 5th Suffolks or the 1/8th Hants. The bodies of three officers were found belonging to the Norfolks, but it was impossible to identify them. I have ordered a special search to be made for Col. Beauchamp.
>
> Two identity discs were found one belonging to Pte. Cattor and the other to Pte. Barnaby with 5th Norfolks but I cannot trace either of them in the card index, in fact there are no records of any men of this battalion here.
>
> My reasons for supposing that the bodies discovered are those of the men who were missing after the action of the 12th Aug. are as follows:-

(1) In Sir Ian Hamilton's dispatches it is stated that they were lost in a forest. The country is the vicinity of the place where the bodies were found is comparatively thickly wooded and is the only area in the Suvla sector which would in any way tally with the description. In addition the farm would be on the frontage allotted to the battalion in the order of battle.

See Note 6.

(2) The spot is half a mile behind the Turkish front lines and I have no record that it was reached on any subsequent occasion or that the three battalions, traces of which have been found, ever made an attack there again.

See Note 5.

(3) According to one account Col. Beauchamp was last seen entering a farm in this area at the head of his men, and nothing further was heard of him. The Turkish occupier of this land has been interviewed and he stated that when he returned to the ruins of his farm after the evacuation it was covered with decomposing bodies of British soldiers which he threw down a small ravine in the immediate neighbourhood. It was in this ravine that many of the bodies were found and it would appear from this that a portion of the battalion were surrounded in the farm and annihilated.

NOTES ON THE GRAVES IN GALLIPOLI.

1. Almost every Grave was desecrated and the Cross or other distinguishing mark destroyed or removed. In some cases the bodies had not been re-interred. This explains the difficulty in finding the graves of those who were known to have been buried. In the case of isolated graves it was frequently impossible.

2. 'Bodies' were only bones and all recognizable uniform decayed. A shoulder title, Regimental crest or badge of rank was often the only means of identification and in many cases even those were absent.

3. The Turk always robbed the dead of everything of value and made a practice of collecting discs. This accounts for the fact that so many are buried as unknown.

4. All remains have now been buried in Graves marked with wooden Crosses. Most of these are in

carefully fenced in Cemeteries.

NOTES ON OFFICIAL REPORT.

5. It is known that A Co. of the 1/5 Norfolks who were on the left of the line went off to silence guns that were causing heavy casualties. The Turkish Farmer also stated that there were big numbers of bodies lying in the open – these had been thrown into a Dere (dry bed which becomes a running stream in rainy season) and so carried away. This is the ground for the opinion that the advance was caught by Machine Gun fire. Identifications were found the order of the advance:-

Left	Centre	Right
5 Suffs.	8 Hants.	5 Norfks.

6. Both our and the Turkish frontline trenches have been advanced since 12th August 1915. The remains were found on land which was never subsequently reached by British Troops and buried with the Church Service on 7th Oct. 1919 by me.

(Signed) C. Pierrepoint Edwards.
Chaplain Ter. Forces.
54th Division.

There is some doubt as to who commissioned this secret report and for that matter why the Rev Edwards was chosen to write it. Officially it was the War office who had sent him. However it is strongly believed that Queen Alexandra and Sir Dighton Probyn, anxious for information about the 5th Norfolks and especially Captain Beck and the Sandringham company, asked the Rev Edwards to return to Gallipoli. Pierrepoint Edwards seemed the perfect choice. We know he had close ties with the Royal Family, he attended a number of Royal occasions, had a horse presented to him by King Edward VII, and that a relative of his, Sir Fleetwood Edwards, was a councillor to both Queen Victoria and Edward VII. He also knew the Gallipoli peninsula well. After Pierrepoint Edwards final report the matter seemed, at last, to have been cleared up and the fate of the 5th Battalion of the Norfolk regiment finally resolved. The story however refused to go away.

25. *Captain Frank Beck's watch, presented to his daughter Margeretta on her wedding day.*

In 1922 news came from the British Military Representative in Smyrna that he had received information regarding the whereabouts of a gold Hunter watch said to have been found on the body of a British officer on a battlefield in Gallipoli. This watch bore an inscription that showed it had been presented by a member of the British Royal Family, believed to be Queen Alexandra, to her friend Sir Dighton Probyn VC and that he had subsequently presented the watch to Capt Beck, agent to the Royal Family on their estate at Sandringham. The watch was found to be in the hands of a former Turkish General Musta Bey, who had been in command of the sector over which the 5th Norfolks attacked. At first Musta Bey demanded £150 for the return of the watch. This offer was rejected by the British authorities. Since Musta Bey wanted to move from Constantinople to Smyrna he agreed that provided he could be guaranteed safe conduct he would take £10 for the watch. The Beck family were later told that it was on the personal insistence of Mustafa Kemal, the first president of modern Turkey, that the watch was handed back to the family. The British afforded travel facilities for Musta Bey and he returned the watch which was forwarded to General Harington, who returned it to Sir Dighton Probyn along with several other items belonging to Capt Beck, including a small pocket knife. Sir Dighton finally presented the watch to Margeretta Beck, Frank Beck's daughter, on her wedding day. It still remains in the Beck family today.

It would have been good to finish the story with the safe return of Capt Beck's watch to the family, but the legend of the Vanished Battalion had several more twists and turns to make before it was finally resolved.

Chapter ten

Strange Clouds

We listened; but we only heard
The feeble chirping of a bird
That starved upon its perch:
And, listening still, without a word,
We set about our hopeless search.

Wilfrid Wilson Gibson (1878-1962)

Probably the strangest account of the disappearance of the 5th Norfolks came on 25 April 1965 during the celebrations in Turkey to commemorate the 50th Anniversary of the Allied Landings in Gallipoli. Mr Frederick Reichardt, who had served throughout the campaign as a sapper with the New Zealand Expeditionary Force, made a remarkable statement, supported by three other veterans who had also been present at the time of the 5th Norfolks' disappearance. Their position, high up on one of the hills that surrounded Suvla Bay, gave the men a good and clear view of what took place during the confusion of the battle. Since that time this statement has been put forward for one reason or another as a 'reasonable' explanation for the battalion's disappearance.

> 21st August 1915
>
> The following is an account of the strange incident that happened on the above date, which occurred in the morning during the severest and final period of fighting which took place on Hill 60. Suvla Bay. ANZAC.
>
> The day broke clear, without a cloud in sight, as any beautiful Mediterranean day could be expected to be. The exception, however, was a number of perhaps six or eight 'loaf of Bread' shaped clouds – all shaped exactly alike, which were hovering over Hill 60. It was noticed that, in spite of a four or five mile an hour breeze from the south, these clouds did not

alter their position in any shape or form, nor did they drift away under the influence of the breeze. They were hovering at an elevation of about 60 degrees as seen from our observation point 500 feet up. Also stationary and resting on the ground right underneath this group of clouds was a similar cloud in shape, measuring about 800 feet in length, 220 feet in height, and 200 feet in width. This cloud was absolutely dense, solid looking in structure, and positioned about 14 to 18 chains from the fighting in British held territory. All this was observed by 22 men of No. 3 Section, No 1 Field Company, N.Z.E., including myself, from our trenches on Rhododendron Spur, approximately 2,500 yards south west of the cloud on the ground. Our vantage point was overlooking Hill 60 by about 300 feet. As it turned out later, this singular cloud was straddling a dry creek bed or sunken road [Kaiajik Derel] and we had a perfect view of the cloud's sides and ends as it rested on the ground. Its colour was a light grey, as was the colour of the other clouds.

A British regiment, the First Fourth Norfolks, of several hundred men, was then noticed marching up this sunken road or creek towards hill 60. However, when they arrived at this cloud, they marched straight into it, with no hesitation, but no one ever came back out to deploy and fight at Hill 60. About an hour later, after the last of the file had disappeared into it, this cloud very unobtrusively lifted off the ground and, like any cloud or fog would, rose slowly until it joined the other similar clouds which were mentioned at the beginning of this account. On viewing them again, they all looked alike 'as peas in a pod.' All this time, the group of clouds had been hovering in the same place, but as soon as the singular cloud had risen to their level, they all moved away northwards, i.e., towards Thrance [Bulgaria]. In a matter of about three-quarters of an hour they had all disappeared from view.

The regiment mentioned is posted as missing or 'wiped out' and on Turkey surrendering in 1918, the first thing Britain demanded of the Turkey was the return of this regiment. Turkey replied that she had neither captured this regiment, nor made contact with it, and did not know it existed. A British Regiment in 1914-18 consisted of any number between 800 and 4,000 men. Those who observed this incident vouch for the fact that Turkey never captured that regiment, nor made contact with it.

We, the undersigned, although late in time, this is the 50th Jubilee of the ANZAC landing declare that the above described incident is true in every word.

Signed by witnesses:

4/165 Sapper F. Reichardt. Matata, Bay of Plenty

13/416 Sapper R. Newnes. 157 King Street, Cambridge

J.L. Newman. 75 Freyberg Street, Octumoctai, Tauranga

Reichardt's fantastic story first appeared in the New Zealand journal *Spaceview* and aroused considerable interest throughout the world. The story next appeared in March 1966 in an issue of the American UFO magazine, *Flying Saucers.* Since this time Reichardt's account of the battalion's disappearance has appeared in numerous books and articles mainly concerning unidentified flying objects, Bermuda triangles and strange disappearances, each putting forward their own bizarre explanations for the loss of the 5th Norfolks. Yet none of these accounts, which is often the case, seems to have examined the facts in full, accepting Reichardt's explanation at face value (besides stories of UFO's and strange disappearances sell more books). If indeed Sapper Reichardt was describing the fate of the 5th battalion, Norfolk Regiment then he made several obvious mistakes.

First Reichardt identifies the wrong battalion, describing them as the 1/4th Norfolks. In fact the fourth battalion were in reserve on the day of the attack and although they were involved in the fighting did not suffer many casualties. It was (as we know) the 1/5th that made the attack and later vanished as they advanced through the burning wood. The date given by Reichardt for the attack was the morning of 21 August 1915, when in fact the events took place in the late afternoon of 12 August 1915. There was indeed a major British attack on 21 August against the Turkish positions, but largely because of the losses they had already sustained the fifth Norfolks took no part in it. Sapper Reichardt and his company were over four and a half miles from the scene of the Norfolks' line of attack and even with binoculars their power of observation must have been phenomenal if they could see through the dust and conditions of a major battle, and identify the units taking part in the attack. We also know that Major (later Lieut-Col) Villiers Stuart had a clear view of the entire battle and certainly didn't see any strange-shaped clouds, and he was writing about the incident in 1932, only 17 years after the Norfolks disappeared, unlike Reichardt who was recounting his experiences fifty years later.

Why then should Reichardt and his colleagues tell such a strange tale? And was it a complete and utter fabrication? I believe that Reichardt was not lying but had become confused. The date on which he alleges that he saw the 5th Norfolks disappear, 21 August 1915, saw the Allies involved in a major offensives against the Turkish positions, involving over 3000 men in an attack on Hill 60. The battle, one of the bloodiest of the campaign, raged for almost a week, ending like most of the Allied offensives with thousands of casualties and total failure. In the smoke and gloom of battle Reichardt could have observed any one of dozens of battalions as they advanced through the mists of battle. Once the story had been told it undoubtedly became embellished with each re-telling and over fifty years the story undoubtedly became totally confused.

The most believable alternative is that Reichardt and his friends saw the Sherwood Rangers Yeomanry as they advanced on Scimitar Hill led by Lieut-Colonel Sir John Peniston Milbank VC. The Sherwood Rangers attacked in total confusion. Colonel Milbank remarked to one of his officers, 'We are to take a redoubt but I don't know where it is, and I don't think anyone else does either; but in any case we are to go ahead and attack any Turks we meet.'

They are reported to have advanced into an evil, swirling, unseasonable mist and were lost to sight. With the Turkish soldiers dug in on the top of the position they were attacking, the Sherwood Rangers were cut to pieces. They attacked at the time and date reported by Reichardt, they also attacked into a swirling mist, with few of the soldiers returning, including Colonel Milbank VC who was killed. It is also significant that both the destruction of the Sherwood Rangers and the disappearance of the 5th Norfolks were reported on facing pages of the 'Final Report', and that the report was declassified in 1965 the very year that Reichardt and his friends told their remarkable story.

Chapter eleven

The Reason Why

I am the man behind it all;
I am the one responsible.

Peter Appleton

Despite the Rev Pierrepoint Edwards' finding the remains of 122 members of the Battalion in a mass grave in 1919, the various stories surrounding the disappearance of the 5th Norfolks continued. It was somehow as if people were not satisfied with the bland conclusion that these men had just, like thousands of other brave soldiers during the Gallipoli campaign, been killed in battle. The stories varied from the interesting to the bizarre. However after Sapper Reichardt's revelations in 1965 and the publicity that surrounded it, the story was once again forgotten. It surfaced again on the 29 July 1973 in the Australian paper the *Sun-Herald* under the headline,

How Did a Complete British Regiment
the First Fifth Norfolks Disappear
on the 28th August 1915?

It continued:

> August 28th was a beautiful clear day, but it was noticed that six or eight 'Loaf of Bread' clouds were hovering over Hill 60 near Suvla Bay. The clouds, despite a strong breeze, did not move. The regiment of several hundred men was seen marching up a sunken road towards Hill 60. The regiment marched into the cloud, one of the clouds hovering over the road, but did not come out.

The article was written as publicity for the book *The Eternal Subject* by Brinsley le Poer Trench. The story was picked up by several British papers and the whole controversy once more reared its head. The Gallipoli Society, an organization dedicated to the memory and history of the campaign, now heartily sick of these bizarre stories, decided to try to end the myths surrounding the battalion once and for all. In their annual magazine the *Gallipolian* they requested any information about the incident from any of their members, many hundreds of which were Gallipoli veterans. Dozens of men replied to the request but none (surprisingly enough) mentioned having seen any strange clouds which might have been UFOs. However amongst the replies was one that began to shed a fresh and rather sinister light on the disappearance of the battalion.

26. *Signaller Gordon Parker* (second from right, in sidecar).

Gordon Parker had been a signaller with the Royal Engineers attached to the 54th division and had been with them in Gallipoli during the time of the battalion's disappearance. He was a straightforward, level-headed man with a good business sense, who after the war became a self-made millionaire. At one time he purchased Felixstowe docks to help solve a business problem over importing and exporting his merchandise. Parker wrote to the

Gallipolian that some years after the war he had met his old friend the Rev Pierrepoint Edwards MC and that they had quite naturally talked about the campaign. The subject of the disappearance of the 5th Norfolks came up and the Rev Edwards told him about the finding of the mass grave containing the remains of many of the Norfolks. He went on, however, to tell him something that had not been included in any report or known conversation before, namely that every man that he had found had been shot in the head. The Rev Edwards had no reason to lie, or exaggerate. His mission had in many ways been a personal crusade to try to find the truth about what befell a group of men for whom he had a great regard. In any attack a certain number of both attacking and defending soldiers might be expected to be shot in the head, but it is beyond belief that it could have happened to all of them.

Despite many stories to the contrary we know that Turkish soldiers did not like taking prisoners. Many of the soldiers during the campaign also knew this. Second-Lieut Pelly noted in his diary after the Norfolks' attack on 12 August that 'The Turks were taking no prisoners!' We also know that at least Capt Pattrick, commanding officer of the Lynn company and one of his sergeants, Ernest Beart, had been seen being disarmed and taken prisoner-of-war, and that neither of these men was ever seen again. Information regarding the treatment of prisoners-of-war by the Turkish army are equally startling. Of the 5,000 men who were lost in the 1st Australian Division only one man was taken prisoner-of-war, many Australian troops knew that to be wounded and captured by the Turkish soldiers meant almost certain death. A good example of the Turkish treatment of prisoners-of-war is illustrated in Lieut John Still's (6th East Yorks) book *A Prisoner of the Turks*. In this book he vividly recalls the circumstances of the death of his commanding officer Lieutenant-Colonel Henry Glanville Allen Moore. He wrote:

> The 6 East Yorks were ordered forward to capture the Tekke Tepe Ridge. The order was received one hour later because the messenger got lost. About thirty men managed to reach the top but were immediately swept off by a larger force of Turks who had just arrived. The battle was lost within about half an hour. The retirement of this little party was attended by heavy loss. Only the commanding officer, two other officers and two men returned to the foothills and here they were

> overpowered and taken prisoner. After surrendering the party was threatened with bayonets and although an Iman (Holy man) tried to stop any killing, Lieut-Coln Moore was bayoneted in cold blood. Still was allowed to tend him, Colonel Moore said that his wound didn't hurt very much and Lieut Still began to carry him towards captivity, but he died soon afterwards. Lieut Still went on to relate a subsequent conversation with a German Officer who told him that they were having great difficulty in getting Turkish soldiers to take prisoners, even if they explained to them that captives were required for intelligence.

Even the one-time American Ambassador in Constantinople, Lewis Einstein, noted when writing about the attitude of the Turkish soldiers towards their enemy, 'One moment they will murder wantonly and the next surprise everybody by their kindness.'

Douglas Stott, who has made a long-term study of the Turkish attitude towards prisoners during the Gallipoli campaign, made the following points:

> The Turks were very reluctant to take prisoners, I don't think they knew they had to and initially they didn't take any, it wasn't their idea of warfare. It was also their first experience of defending their own soil, they rose to the occasion and they proved themselves to be first class infantrymen. They also hated Europeans; Europeans who had looked down on them, treated them at times like dirt, particularly in Sinai and Mesopotamia and when a soldier was captured they became very agitated and excited, in may ways uncontrollable, at times almost running amok.

There are no reliable figures for the total British and Dominion prisoners taken by the Turks during the Gallipoli campaign. The most accurate appraisal probably comes from the American ambassador in a communication prepared in February 1916, who put the total at approximately 490, of which at least ninety-six later died in captivity. Most of the other ranks were transferred to various work camps on the notorious Analotia railway and it was in these camps that the high proportion of deaths occurred as a result of the inhuman conditions imposed by their captors. In the early 1920s the remains of these unfortunate souls, where they could be located, were gathered in and individually re-interred in plot XXI,

Baghdad (North Gate) War Cemetery. Those that could not be found are commemorated on special memorials in the same cemetery.

The most telling evidence only came to light in 1991 however when Mrs Madge Webber, the sister-in-law of Arthur Webber, told her remarkable story, on the BBC2 programme *All the King's Men*, for the first time since Arthur told her many years before. Private Arthur Webber had been wounded in the face and taken prisoner-of-war while serving with the Yarmouth Company of the 5th Norfolks during the battle on 12 August 1915. After the death of his wife he became close to his sister-in-law and finally told her his secret; a secret he had kept for over seventy-five years.

> Arthur Webber was a member of the Territorials and when the 1914-18 war broke out of course he had to go, I think he wanted to go in any case like all the young men of that time. When they were first called up they met in Dereham and they eventually heard they were going to the Dardanelles. When they heard they were going abroad I don't suppose they knew where they were going but they ended up at the Dardanelles and he was in the landings in early August 1915 and they had a very fierce fight but they were overwhelmed, he went into a wood, they were fighting in a wood and he was shot through the face. It went into his cheek bone on one side of his face and came out of the other breaking his jaw. He fell to the ground wounded and unable to speak, everything around him was on fire but he was helpless. After a while everything went quiet and he realised that the battle was over. Then he heard the Turkish soldiers coming along and they were collecting the dead and shooting and bayoneting the wounded and the prisoners. A Turkish soldier came up to Arthur and stuck a bayonet in him which went into his thigh he was just about to do it again when a German officer appeared on the scene and said, 'That man is not dead and must be taken prisoner-of-war.' Arthur realised what a marvellously lucky escape he had in all this carnage.

By a strange quirk of fate Arthur Webber's life was saved by a German officer (not the only example of German officers saving British and Commonwealth lives during the campaign). As a prisoner-of-war Arthur was taken on a nine day journey over the rough Turkish landscape into captivity in Constantinople. He received first class medical attention from German doctors who repaired his shattered jaw. After regaining his strength he was sent to work on the infamous Turus railway tunnel through which the Germans and Turkish military planned to run men and munitions to the front, but which was later blown up by Lawrence of Arabia. After the war Arthur continued working for the family engineering firm of Arthur H. Webber and Sons Ltd in Yarmouth which was established in 1889 and still operates today. He finally died in December 1969 aged eighty-six years, still with the Turkish sniper's bullet in his head but fortunately not before telling his fascinating story.

Chapter twelve

A Final Farewell

If we return, will England be
Just England still to you and me?
The place where we must earn our bread
We, who have walked among the dead.

F.W. Harvey

There can be little doubt that there was nothing extra-terrestrial about the disappearance of the 5th Norfolks. The disaster that befell the battalion was undoubtedly a combination of incompetence by the commanding officers like Sir Ian Hamilton and the bravery of a green battalion determined to prove itself.

The battalion, fresh from England and with no experience under enemy fire, was forced to attack across land that had not been reconnoitred and with maps that were less than useless. They advanced towards a determined enemy, well positioned and concealed, in broad daylight, not even sure of their final objective. They were led by a colonel who, although fearless, had little experience or understanding of leading infantry in battle, and whose idea of an attack was to keep advancing no matter what the cost or position of the enemy. As a result the battalion was surrounded and cut to pieces. Had it not been for the quick thinking of Evelyn Beck in stopping the vast majority of the men from following Colonel Beauchamp through the wood, the disaster would have been far worse. Thankfully most of the battalion managed to withdraw to the safety of their own lines, or fought their way through the Turkish positions. Those who were left behind, wounded or unable to retreat, were either killed on the spot by an enemy under siege and reluctant to take prisoners or, thanks to a German Officer, taken prisoner-of-war.

Why then did the story of the 5th battalion cause so much controversy, both at the time and for the next seventy-five years? Thousands of men had disappeared into the heat and dust of the Gallipoli campaign: members of the House of Lords, members of parliament, the sons and husbands of gentry and the influential, yet despite this it was the loss of the 5th Norfolks which was to give rise to such debate and mystery. Quite simply it was the presence, amongst their ranks, of Capt Frank Beck and the Sandringham company. As we know, shortly after the battle King George V telegraphed Sir Ian Hamilton enquiring about the fate of the company. This enquiry must seriously have disturbed Hamilton. What was he to say – 'Sorry but I've just sacrificed them all quite needlessly in yet another botched attack in Suvla'! His best course of action, I believe, was to create an air of mystery about the whole incident and thereby with luck stop any form of enquiry into their loss or his leadership. The men had, for the time anyway, only been reported 'missing' and therefore there was still hope that some might be alive. Keeping matters uncertain kept his critics at arm's length. In the end it mattered little, for a few months later Sir Ian Hamilton was relieved of his command and was never to be offered another.

In 1919 when the Rev Pierrepoint Edwards MC chanced upon the remains of 122 members of the battalion, he compiled a report that neglected to mention the fact that all the men found in the mass grave had been shot in the head. The press was allowed to publish extracts of the official report stating that they had all been killed gallantly in action, 'face to face with the enemy'. The Rev Pierrepoint Edwards, who was close to the Royal Family and well aware of their distress – particularly Queen Alexandra's at the loss of so many of their friends and estate workers – must have thought it pointless for the Royal Family or the men's friends and relations to rake up the past and cause any further anguish. It is for that reason, I am convinced, that he never spoke of it again, until he told his old friend Gordon Parker, who also kept the secret until shortly before his death. The combination of an initial cover-up and a regard for the feelings of the men's families and friends allowed the mystery to continue for seventy-five years, and a series of bizarre tales to develop and grow.

As for the battalion, after the battle on 12 August they remained in Gallipoli for the duration of the campaign. They had been so badly decimated that they took no further part in major actions. On 22 September 1915, command of the battalion was taken over by Lieut-Colonel Kinsman of the 4th Inniskillings and finally on 4 December the Norfolks were evacuated from the peninsula and embarked for Mudros. Of the original officers who accompanied the battalion to Gallipoli, only three remained: Capt Eustace Cubitt (who had become the battalion's adjutant), Capt Evelyn Beck MC and Major Buxton. (Capt Birkbeck was also in the peninsula but had left the battalion to become an embarkation officer.) It was said that the British army's greatest achievement during the campaign was the evacuation of the peninsula. From Mudros the battalion was transferred to Egypt and camped at the foot of of the Great Pyramids. After being reinforced, the battalion next saw action in Palestine where once again they were thrown into an ill-prepared attack and were slaughtered, losing over 200 men in a single day, including many of those that had survived the Gallipoli campaign. Among them was Eustace Cubitt, the last of the Cubitt brothers, Evelyn Beck MC who had saved so many of the Norfolks by not advancing into the wood and Capt Birkbeck who had returned to the battalion to be close to his friends.

After training so hard for years, the Norfolks marched off to war in 1914 with high hopes only to be decimated in two days of battle suffering losses from which they never fully recovered. As for the fourteen prisoners taken by the Turks on 12 August, five died later in captivity, causing a double anguish for their families.

All over Norfolk on small and large memorials alike are the names of the men from the Vanished Battalion. In October 1920, in a ceremony attended by King George V, Queen Alexandra and Queen Mary, a cross was unveiled on the greensward outside Sandringham Church bearing the names of all those men from the estate who died during the Great War. In a line one above the other are the names of Frank, Alec and Evelyn Beck, still together on the Sandringham estate. Later the Royal Family placed a brass plaque inside the church at Sandringham commemorating Capt Frank Beck. It reads:

TO THE MEMORY OF
CAPTAIN FRANK REGINALD BECK M.V.O.
5th NORFOLK REGT
AND IN GRATEFUL REMEMBRANCE OF 25 YEARS FAITHFUL
SERVICE AS LAND AGENT OF THE SANDRINGHAM ESTATES
TO KING EDWARD VII, QUEEN ALEXANDRA & KING GEORGE V.
KILLED IN ACTION GALLIPOLI DURING THE GREAT WAR

ON AUGUST 12th 1915.
AGED 54 YEARS.

The plaque is situated close to another commemorating Frank Beck's father, Edmund. They sit comfortably together with a number of other memorials to members of the Royal Family: King Edward VII, King George V and Queen Alexandra. The estate workers, also keen to show their appreciation and respect for Frank Beck and the other men who had left Sandringham in 1914 never to return, dedicated a stained-glass window in the parish church at West Newton, into which are engraved the words: 'To the glory of God and in proud and loving memory of Captain Frank Beck MVO and his men.'

27. *The Helles Memorial.*

Over 3,000 miles away on a cliffside overlooking the Aegean Sea stands the Helles Memorial, an obelisk over thirty metres high and clearly visible to ships as they pass through the Dardanelles. Inscribed on it are the names of over 20,000 men who have no known graves or who were lost or buried at sea. On a tablet at the front of the memorial, looking out over the sea that brought them to Gallipoli, are the names of the officers and men of the 5th Norfolks who made the supreme sacrifice during the fighting for the inhospitable peninsula, together again for the last time.

Perhaps it would be best to give the final word to Mustafa Kemal, the great president and leader of the Turkish people:

> Those heros that shed their blood and lost their lives... You are now lying in the soil of a friendly country. Therefore rest in peace. There is no difference between the Johnnies and the Mehmets to us where they lie side by side here in this country of ours ...
>
> You, the mothers who sent your sons from far away countries, wipe away your tears; your sons are lying in our bosom and are in peace.

MY OFFICER

My Officer was a vicar's son,
He was lean, he was brave
And like a soldier he proudly won
His mother's heart to save,
Then out to Gallipoli was his call
Where shells and bullets screamed
But my Officer remained steadfast and calm
For this moment – he had dreamed.

As we advanced we were all as one
And we knew the battle was on,
With our bayonets fixed we all prayed
As did the vicar's son,
We knew the Turks had us covered well
But on and on we ran,
Then suddenly my Officer wounded fell
Upon Gallipoli's scorching sand.

And as I knelt to dress his wounds
He told me to press on
But I knew my Officer had heard death's sound
As had many a mother's son,
The Norfolk lads had played their part
As indeed all soldiers can
But through the fallen, and broken hearts,
Peace must always stand.

Pte T. Williamson

Appendix I

Officers that Travelled with the 1/5th Norfolks to Gallipoli

Lieut-Colonel Sir Horace George Proctor-Beauchamp (6th Bart) (C.B.). Killed in action, Gallipoli, 12 August 1915.

Majors:
W.J. Barton.
T.W. Purdy. Wounded in action, 12 August 1915.

Captains:
A.E. Ward (Adjutant). Killed in action, Gallipoli, 12 August 1915.
F.R. Beck, M.V.O. (Commanding Officer Sandringham Company). Killed in action, Gallipoli, 12 August 1915.
A.D. Pattrick (Commanding Officer Lynn Company). Killed in action, Gallipoli, 12 August 1915.
A. Wright, M.V.O.
E.R. Cubitt. Killed in action, Gallipoli, 12 August 1915.
A.G. Coxon. Prisoner-of-war, Gallipoli, 12 August 1915.
A.H. Mason. Killed in action, Gallipoli, 12 August 1915.
E.R. Woodwark. Killed in action, Gallipoli, 12 August 1915.

Lieutenants:
T. Oliphant. Wounded in action, 12 August 1915.
E.A. Beck. M.C. Killed in action, Palestine, 19 April 1917.
G.W. Birkbeck. Killed in action, Palestine, 19 April 1917.
E. Gay. Killed in action, Gallipoli, 12 August 1915.
V.M. Cubitt. Killed in action, Gallipoli, 12 August 1915.
E.H. Cubitt. Killed in action, Palestine, 19 April 1917.
A.G. Culme-Seymore. Wounded in action, 12 August 1915.

Second-Lieutenants:
R. Burroughs. Killed in action, Gallipoli, 12 August 1915.

M.B.G. Beauchamp. Killed in action, Gallipoli, 12 August 1915.
A.E. Beck, M.C. Killed in action, Gallipoli, 12 August 1915.
A. Beck.
A. R. Pelly. Wounded in action, Gallipoli, 12 August 1915.
M.F. Oliphant. Killed in action, Gallipoli, 12 August 1915.
R. Adams. Killed in action, Gallipoli, 12 August 1915.
W.G.S. Fawkes. Prisoner-of-war, 12 August 1915.
W. C. James.
M.B. Buxton.
Q.M. Hon Lte S. Parker. Died of wounds, 1 November 1915.
M.O. Captain R.G. Laden.

Appendix II

Casualties (other ranks) 1/5th Norfolks, 12 August 1915

e. Enlisted
b. Born

1. Allen, George, 1136, Pte, b.Aylsham, e. Aylsham.
2. Atto, Hubert Ernest, 2484, Pte, e. East Dereham.
3. Baker, Sidney, 2206, Pte, b. Gt Yarmouth, e. Gt Yarmouth.
4. Balls, Horace, 2245, Pte, b. Norwich, e. Norwich.
5. Barber, John, 2622, Pte, e. Dereham.
6. Barker, George Herbert, 2308, Pte, e. East Dereham.
7. Barnaby, John Augustus, 240436, Cpl. e. East Dereham.
8. Barnes, Richard, 1877, Pte, b. Wood Dalling. e. Aylsham.
9. Beart, Ernest William, 2185, A/SGT b. Downham Market. e. East Dereham.
10. Beck, Leonard, 3133, Pte, e. Gt Yarmouth.
11. Beckett, Frederick George, 1758, Pte, b. St Nicholas. e. Gt Yarmouth.
12. Belding, Frederick Ernest, 2416, Pte, e. East Dereham.
13. Bentley, Joseph William, 3411, Pte, e. East Dereham.
14. Beresford, Robert William, 293, Sgt. b. Holt. e. Holt.
15. Bircham, William, 1549, Pte, b. Brampton, e. Buxton.
16. Blyth, Reginald Henry, 1692, Pte, b. St Nicholas. e. Gt Yarmouth.
17. Bond, William James, 2418, Pte, e. East Dereham.
18. Bowles, Sidney Robert, 2757, Pte, b. Gt Yarmouth. e. Gt Yarmouth.
19. Brand, Charles Agnew, 3081, L/Cpl. e. Gt Yarmouth.
20. Bridges, Leonard Arthur, 3335, Pte, e. East Dereham.
21. Britton, Alfred Robert, 2968, Pte, e. East Dereham.
22. Bullimore, Cecil Ernest, 1432, Pte, b. Westwick, N. Walsham. e. Norwich.
23. Bushell, George John Charles, 1306, Pte, b. St Wickelwood, e. Gt Yarmouth.

24. Bussey, Ernest Edward, 1387, Pte, b. Briston, e. Melton Constable.
25. Butcher, George William Reynolds, 3436, Pte, b. Litcham. e. East Dereham.
26. Carter, Sidney, 1555, Pte, b. Shouldham. e. West Newton.
27. Carter, Walter, 1028, Pte, b. Wretton. e. Stoke Ferry.
28. Chamberlin, Walter. 2520, Pte, e. Aylsham.
29. Chapman, John Arthur, 3780, b. Moulton St Mary, Gt Yarmouth, e. Dereham.
30. Christopherson, Clifford Bunting, 2988, Pte, e. Dereham.
31. Codling, Harry, 1879, Pte, b. Hindolvestone, e. Aylsham.
32. Cowen, William Charles, 1129, L/Sgt, b. St Margaret's Lynn, e. King's Lynn.
33. Cox, Edgar Samuel, 1376, Pte, b. Wolferton, e. Sandringham.
34. Crake, Bert, 2522, Pte, e. Dereham.
35. Crammer, Ernest, 77, Sgt, b. East Dereham, e. East Dereham.
36. Craske, Victor Cyril, 1447. Pte, b. Sheringham, e. Sheringham.
37. Crowe, Charles, 2524, Pte, e. East Dereham.
38. Curtis, Wilfred Sidney, 2312, Pte, b. Cotton, e. East Dereham.
39. Deacon, James Lewis, 3383, Pte, e. East Dereham.
40. Dodson, Samuel Daniel, 2210, Pte, b. Gt Yarmouth, e. Gt Yarmouth.
41. Doughty, Donald Ernest, 2273, Pte, b. Downham Market, e. East Dereham.
42. Dove, Robert George, 819, Cpl, b. Harlesdon Norfolk, e. Sandringham.
43. Durrant, Arthur, 2472, Pte, e. Gt Yarmouth.
44. Eassom, Arthur, 2654, L/Cpl, e. East Dereham.
45. Eglen, Isiah, 2652, Pte, e. East Dereham.
46. Emmerson, Ernest, 2129, A/Cpl, b. Dersingham, e. Dersingham.
47. Fenton, Frank, 1411, L/Cpl, b. Thornham, e. Thornham.
48. Field, Herbert Joseph, 2490. Cpl, e. Gt Yarmouth.
49. Forsythe, Robert Edward, 1881, Pte, b. Finchley, Middx, e. Gt Yarmouth.
50. Fox, Albert Levi, 1950, Pte, b. Raynham. e, Fakenham.
51. Franklin, Harry, 2865, Pte, e. Gt Yarmouth.
52. Franklin, Herbert Thomas, 1571, Pte, b. Swaffham, e. Swaffham.
53. Franklin, Leonard, 1706, Pte, b. Watlington, e. Downham. Norfolk.
54. Futter, Arthur Robert, 4298, Pte, e. Gt Yarmouth.
55. Gallant, Walter, 2192, Pte, b. Gt Yarmouth, e. Gt Yarmouth.
56. Gedge, Bertie, 2473, Pte, b. St Nicholas, Gt Yarmouth, e. Gt Yarmouth.
57. Goreham, William, 1600, Pte, b. Fakenham, e. Fakenham. Norfolk.
58. Goulder, John Lee, 2179, Sgt, b. Aylsham, e. Aylsham.
59. Greenwood, John Beckett, 3327, Pte, e. East Dereham.

60. Greeves, George, 3296, Pte, e. East Dereham.
61. Griffin, George, 1768, Cpl, b. Gayton, e. Gayton.
62. Griston, Geoffrey Joseph, 2575, Pte, e. East Dereham.
63. Groom, Arnold, 1118, A/Cpl, b. Fakenham, e. Fakenham.
64. Groom, Walter, 2765, Pte, e. East Dereham.
65. Grummitt, George Ernest, 2673, Pte, e. East Dereham.
66. Hacon, Herbert George, 2576, Pte, e. Gt Yarmouth.
67. Hall, Bertie, 1702, Pte, b. Hilgay, e. Downham Market.
68. Halls, Robert Henry, 2491, Pte, e. Gt Yarmouth.
69. Harbage, Edwin George, 2579, Pte, e. East Dereham.
70. Harnwell, George, 2125, Pte, b. Downham Market, e. Downham Market.
71. Hellenburgh, Arthur Robert, 1564, Pte, b. St Nicholas Yarmouth, e, Gt Yarmouth.
72. Heron, Frederick George, 3022, Pte, e. East Dereham.
73. Heseltine, Frank, 2679, Pte, e. East Dereham.
74. Hey, Charles William, 3503, Pte, e. East Dereham.
75. Holman, Harry, 1441, Pte, b. Fordham, e. Downham Market.
76. Howell, Ernest, 3031, Pte, e. East Dereham.
77. Howell, Henry, 1898, A/Cpl, b. East Dereham, e. East Dereham.
78. Hubbard, Harry, 2152, Pte, b. Wereham, e. Downham Market.
79. Humphrey, William John, 1523, Pte, b. Grimston, e. Flitcham.
80. Humphrey, Wilfred Lyal, 2683, Pte, e. Dereham.
81. Hunter, Charles, 321, L/Cpl, b. N. Pickenham, e. Hillington.
82. Johnson, Russell Charles, 2212, L/Cpl. b. Gt Yarmouth, e. Gt Yarmouth.
83. Kerrison, Frederick Robert James, 1751, Pte, b. Walworth Surrey, e. Sandringham.
84. Leggett, Henry Francis, 2348, L/Cpl b. Gt Yarmouth, e. Gt Yarmouth.
85. Lines, Robert, 2880, Pte, e. Dereham.
86. Long, Herbert, 1688, Pte, b. Blakeney, e. Wells.
87. Lovett, Jesse Ernest, 2177, Pte, b. East Dereham, e. East Dereham.
88. Lyon, Ernest, 1960, Pte, b. South Lynn, e. King's Lynn.
89. Macdonald, Frederick, 2267, L/Cpl, b. Gt Yarmouth, e. Gt Yarmouth.
90. Manning, William, 1573, Pte, b. Rougham, e. Swaffham.
91. Marsters, Eric, 2442, Pte, e. East Dereham.
92. McLean, Percy Douglas, 2583, L/Cpl, e. East Dereham.
93. Medlock, Ernest, 1764, Pte, b. Gayton, e. Gayton Norfolk.
94. Meggitt, Richard Dring, 1622, Pte, b. St Margaret's, e. King's Lynn.
95. Miller, George Stanley, 2867, Pte, b. St Nicholas, Gt Yarmouth, e. Gt Yarmouth.
96. Missin, Joseph, 2173, Pte, b. Southery, e. Downham Market.
97. Murrell, Wallace, 2976, Pte, e. East Dereham.

98. Needs, George William, 711, L/Sgt, b. King's Lynn, e. West Newton.
99. Nurse, Robert Wallace, 2130, Pte, b. North Heigham, e. Dersingham.
100. Page, Walter, 1484, Pte, b. St Nicholas, Gt Yarmouth, e. Gt Yarmouth.
101. Parmenter, William Richard, 2198, L/Cpl, b. Stratford, Essex, e. Gt Yarmouth.
102. Payne, William Thomas, 2843, Pte, e. Dereham.
103. Phillips, Fred Ernest, 2025, L/Cpl, b. Icklingham, Suffolk, e. Sandringham.
104. Pike, Lacey, 2588, Pte, e. Dereham.
105. Plaice, Bertie, 2715, Pte, e. Dereham.
106. Porter, Harold Chadwick, 2550, L/Cpl, e. Gt Yarmouth.
107. Ransom, Herbert Charles, 2193, Pte, b. Gt Yarmouth, e. Gt Yarmouth.
108. Reed, Roland Walter Wilfred, 4183, Pte, e. East Dereham.
109. Reeve, Charles, 2723, Pte, e. East Dereham.
110. Reynolds, Frederick James, 2722, Pte, e. East Dereham.
111. Ringer, Roland Edward, 1599, Pte, b. West Newton, e. Sandringam.
112. Rix, Herbert William, 3487, Pte, e. East Dereham.
113. Rix, Walter George, 1895, Pte, b. Cambridge, e. Wells.
114. Robinson, Thomas, 1262, Sgt, b. Cromer, e. Cromer.
115. Rudd, George, 1379, Pte, b. Hardley, e. Aylsham.
116. Rutland, Arthur Edward, 2104, Pte, b. South Lynn, e. King's Lynn.
117. Self, Thomas, 1424, A/Cpl, b. Worstead, e. Westwick.
118. Shickle, Lewis Frank, 2398, L/Cpl, e. East Dereham.
119. Simpson, William Charles, 442, Sgt, b. N. Walsham, e. N. Walsham.
120. Smith, Frank Henry, 2399, Pte, e. East Dereham.
121. Smith, Fredrick William, 2731, Pte, e. East Dereham.
122. Smith, George Thomas, 2459, Sgt, e. East Dereham.
123. Spooner, George, 3473, Pte, e. East Dereham.
124. Spreekley, Frederick Alan, 2412, Pte, e. East Dereham.
125. Stevens, Sidney James, 2598, Pte, e. East Dereham.
126. Theobald, Maurice Jeremiah, 2614, L/Cpl, b. Langford, e. East Dereham.
127. Thompson, Arthur Ernest, 2389, Pte, e. East Dereham.
128. Tipple, Robert James, 1649, L/Cpl, b. Thornham, e. Thornham.
129. Trenowath, Willie, 2413, L/Cpl, e. East Dereham.
130. Tubby, Alfred, 1519, L/Cpl., b. Gorleston, e. Gt Yarmouth.
131. Tuck, William Randall, 2284, L/Cpl, b. Nordelph, e. East Dereham.
132. Turner, Benjamin Robert, 869, Sgt, b. Aylsham, e. Aylsham Norfolk.
133. Wagg, Bertie, 1904, Pte, b. Hunstanton, e. Hunstanton.

134. Wake, Hezekiah Walter, 240037, Cpl, b. Helhoughton, e. East Rudham Norfolk.
135. Walden, Morris Malett, 2385, Pte, b. Dersingham, e. East Dereham Norfolk.
136. Walker, William, 2842, Pte, e. East Dereham.
137. Wellsman, Cyril, 2749, Pte, e. East Dereham.
138. Westgate, Ambrose Henry, 1565, Pte, b. Gt Yarmouth, e. Gt Yarmouth.
139. Whitby, Albert Watson, 1884, Cpl, b. Gt Massingham, e. Gt Massingham.
140. Wilson, William John, 2752, L/Cpl, e. East Dereham.
141. Winter, Ernest William Read, 2616, L/Cpl, b. King's Lynn, e. East Dereham.
142. Woolner, Leslie George, 1837, Pte, b. Hethersett e. Melton Constable.

Appendix III

1/5th Norfolk Regiment Territorials
Prisoners-of-War during Gallipoli Campaign

Angora Internment Camp
Capt Cedric A.M. Coxon.
Capt. William G.S. Fawkes.

Kiangri Internment Camp

1870 (240148)	Sgt. Alfred Allan. d. 22 January 1917. Angora Memorial.
2513	Cpl. William Blott.
1585 (240074)	L/Cpl. Frank N. Fox. d. 4 April 1917. Angora Memorial
3357	Pte. Arthur Edward Brown.
2860	Pte. Charles Ducker.
3043	Pte. Frederick Hooks. d. 18 October 1916. Plot XXI.
2468 (240370)	Pte. Harry Nobbs. d. 22 April 1917. Angora Memorial.
2410	Pte. Alfred Reeve.
3155	Pte. Clifford R. Stairman.
2120	Pte. Donald Swan.
2558 (240410)	Pte. Robert Thompson. d. 21 October 1916. Plot XXI.
3363	Pte. Arthur Webber.

Bibliography

Published Sources:

Brig-Gen C.F. Aspinall-Oglander: *Official History of the War, Military Operations, Gallipoli*

Arthur Banks: *A Military Atlas of the First World War*

C.E.W. Bean: *The Official History of Australia in the War*; Vols 1 & 2

Paul Begg: *Into Thin Air*

Tim Carew: *The Royal Norfolk Regiment*

CWGC Cemetery Registers, Gallipoli

Dragon School Old Boys & Masters who gave their lives in the Great War

Gerald Gliddon: *Norfolk & Suffolk in the Great War*

Robert Graves: *Poems About War*

HMSO: *Officers Died in the Great War 1914-19*

HMSO: *Soldiers Died in the Great War 1914-19 (Norfolk Regt)*

Selected by Edward Hudson: *Poetry of the First World War*

Brig. E.A. James: *British Infancy Regiments 1914-18*

Journals of the Orders and Medals Research Society

Peter Liddle: *Men of Gallipoli*

Memorials of Rugbieans who fell in the Great War

Alan Moorehead: *Gallipoli*

F. Loraine Petre: *The Norfolk Regiment 1685-1918*

The Proprietor: *The Bond of Sacrifice*

Robert Rhodes James: *Gallipoli*

The Marquis De Ruvigny: *The Roll of Honour*

Rob Walker: *Recipients of the Distinguished Conduct Medal 1914-20 (Norfolk Regiment)*

R.W. Walker: *To What Ends Did They Die?*

Ray Westlake: *The Territorial Forces 1914*

Tom Williamson: *The Day the Hills Caught Fire*

J.M. Winter: *The Experience of World War One*

Wykehamists who died in the Great War

Newspapers:
Globe; Sphere; Graphic; The Illustrated London News; Eastern Daily Press; Cromer Post; Cromer Weekly Press; Dereham Times; Diss Express; Diss Journal; Downham Market Gazette; Norwich Evening News; Norwich Weekly Press; Lynn Advertiser; Lynn News; Norfolk Chronicle; Norfolk News; Norwich Mercury; People's Journal (Norwich); *Thetford Times; Thetford Standard; Yarmouth Independent; Yarmouth Mercury; Yarmouth Standard; Yarmouth Times; Yarmouth Weekly Press; Territorial Service; Territorial Gazette; Volunteer T.C. Gazette; The Times.*

Unpublished Sources:
Diary of Major Purdy; Diary and letters of Lieut R. Pelly; Letters of Captain Randall Cubitt; Letters of Captain Victor Cubitt; Letters of Captain Eustace Cubitt; Letters of Captain Frank Beck; Letters of Lieut E. Beck; Letters and telegrams from HRH King George V; Letters and telegrams from Sir Deighton Probyn VC; Letters and telegrams from R. Ridley Mayor of King's Lynn; Letters from Major Woodwark; Letters and diaries, from numerous members of the battalion's rank and file.

Index

Adams, Second-Lieut Robert; 31, 42, 76
Alexandra, HRH Queen; 8, 10, 96, 107, 109, 121, 122
Allen, Sergt; 73
Anafarta Saga (Gallipoli); 68
Aquitania, SS; 56, 57, 58, 59, 60, 103
Azamak Cemetery; 2, 104

Barnaby, John Augustus; 104
Barton, Major; 77
Batchelor's Cottage; 9, (*see also York Cottage*)
Batterbee family; 26, 36
Beales, Lance-Corpl DGM; 76, 100
Beart, Sergt Ernest; 74, 116
Beck, Lieut Albert Edward Alexander (Alec) MC; 28, 31, 41, 87, 90, 98, 100
Beck, Lieut Arthur Evelyn MC; 28, 31, 86, 90, 100, 120, 122
Beck, Edmund; 10, 11, 123
Beck, Capt Frank; 1, 5, 11, 23, 28, 31, 38, 40, 41, 42, 44, 45, 47-8, 63, 66, 71, 74, 75, 98, 107, 109, 122, 123
Beck, Margaretta; 109
Beck, Arthur; 87, 91
Bentley, Private Joseph William; 92, 93, 100
Bey, General Musta; 109
Blott, Corporal; 86
Blott, Private William; 94, 135
Birkbeck, Capt Gervase William; 65, 76, 80, 122
Braithwaite, General; 95
Bridgwater, Capt; 64
Brooke, Rupert; 53
Brown, Private; 73
Brusher, Brigadier; 71
Burroughes, Second-Lieut Randall; 32, 66, 74, 99
Burroughes, Thomas Henry; 10, 31
Buxton, Lieut MB; 122

Carr, Pte George; 5, 75
Carington, Sir William; 40
Catter, Pte; 104
Cann, Pte George; 91
Cheshire Regiment; 2, 19, 104
Churchill, Sir Winston; 50, 101
Cowles, Sergt; 93
Cowper, Charles Spencer; 8
Coxon, Capt Cedric; 34, 46, 75, 94
Crabb, George; 7
Cranmer, Sergt Ernest; 70
Cubitt, Capt Edward Randall; 31, 32, 40, 44, 73, 74, 80, 88, 98, 99
Cubitt, Lieut Eustace; 32, 42, 80, 122
Cubitt, Thomas; 99
Cubitt, Lieut Victor; 31, 42, 60, 80, 98, 99
Culme-Seymore, Capt, AG; 79, 80, 82

Darby, Corp; 79
Davies, Chaplain; 82
Dawson, Pte; 73
Dines, Band Master; 46
Doggett, Private Arnold; 98
Dye, Pte John; 63, 75

Eassom, Lance-Corp; 99
Edward VII, HRH King; 8, 9, 10, 20, 23, 24, 107
Edwards, Rev Charles Pierrepont MC; 103, 104, 105, 107, 114, 116, 121
Edwards, Sir Fleetwood; 107
Einstein, Lewis; 117
Ellett, Scout Wilfred; 75
Essex Regiment; 81

Fawkes, Capt William GS; 73, 95
Foster, Corp; 92, 93
Francis, Pte Albert; 76
Frost, Pte William; 93

Gay, Capt Edmund; 33, 42, 61, 63, 80
George V, HRH King; 1, 9, 10, 44, 48,

89, 91, 95, 98, 99, 121, 122
Goulder, Sergt John; 66, 77, 82
Green, Corp Bertie Ernest; 79
Grimes family; 10, 36

Haldane, Lord; 20, 21
Hamilton, Sir Ian; 1, 43, 54, 68, 70, 89, 90, 91, 95, 120
8th Hampshire Regt; 2, 5, 61, 64, 70, 72, 76, 104
Harington, General; 109
Harrison, Private Cliff; 63, 75
Hoste, James; 8

Jakeman, Sergt Thomas; 76
Jarvis, Signaller; 76
Jay, Pte Leslie; 92
Johnson, Corp; 73

Kemal Mustafa; 56, 109, 124
Kennedy, Major; 79
Kinsman, Lieut-Coln; 121
Knight, Capt Anthony; 44, 67, 68, 71, 76, 77, 82

Lockwood, Pte Julian; 76

Mary, HRH Queen; 9, 10, 122
Mason, Capt Arthur Humfrey; 33, 38, 42, 73, 82
Matthews, Sergt; 93
Medlock, Pte; 73
Meggitt family; 36
Milbank, Lieut-Coln Sir John Peniston VC; 113
Montgomerie, Capt (4th Norfolks); 72
Moore, Lieut-Coln Henry Glanville Allen; 116, 117

Newman, Pte; JL; 112
Newnes, Sapper R; 112
4th Norfolks; 71, 72
Nurse family; 36

Oliphant, Lieut Marcus; 33, 74
Oliphant, Lieut Trevor; 33, 76

Page, The Hon Walter H; 96, 97
Parker, Signaller Gordon; 115, 116, 121
Pattrick, Capt Arthur Devereux; 34, 46, 68, 74, 80, 98, 116
Pearson, Pte Alfred; 74
Pelly, Second-Lieut Rolland; 31, 45, 46, 60, 62, 78, 79, 83, 116
Phipps, Sir Charles; 8
Ponsonby, Sir Frederick; 47, 48
Price, Sir Robert, MP; 95
Probyn, Sir Dighton; 29, 79, 96, 97, 107, 109
Proctor-Beauchamp, Second-Lieut Montague Barclay Granville; 28, 76,
Proctor-Beauchamp, Lieut-Coln Sir Horace George; 25, 42, 43, 46, 70, 71, 82, 104, 120
Purdy, Major Thomas W; 36, 65, 67, 71, 78, 80, 81

Reichardt, Sapper Frederick; 110, 112, 113, 114
Reyce, Robert; 5
Ridley, Mayor of King's Lynn; 83
Rogers, Pte Frank; 36
Rowe, Pte Walter; 58-9

Saul, Pte Herbert; 75
Seaman, Lance-Corp; 65
Smith, Quarter-Master Sergt; 61, 66
Stamfordham, Lord; 43
Stott, Douglas; 117
Still, Lieut John; 116
Suddenham, Sergt Walter; 70
5th Suffolks; 2, 64, 67, 72, 83, 104
Swan, Buglar Donald; 74, 135

Tekke Tepe (Gallipoli); 2, 68
Thrower, Lance-Corp; 68
Tubbenham, Sergt; 75
Tubby, Pte; 74

Victoria, HRH Queen; 107
Villiers-Stuart, Lieut-Coln; 72, 73, 112

Ward, Capt Arthur Edward Martyr; 33, 38, 42, 46, 70, 78, 81
Webber, Pte Arthur Thomas; 94, 118, 119, 135
Webber, Madge; 118
Wells, Sergt-Major; 67
Wigram, Coln Clive; 90
Williamson, Pte Tom; 35, 38, 44, 46, 74, 87, 88
Wolferton, Village; 8
Woodwark, Major; 34, 42, 45, 49, 58, 74

York Cottage; 9, 11, 29